THE CHURCH AND THE
FREE MARKET

THE CHURCH AND THE FREE MARKET

Dilemmas in church welfare agencies accepting contracts from government

Brian Howe

Paul Oslington

Ray Cleary

Marilyn Webster

With questions for group discussion

Edited by Alan Nichols and Maureen Postma

Victorian Council of Churches
Australian Theological Forum

Victorian Council of Churches

Text copyright ' 2002 the authors and the Victorian Council of
Churches for all papers in this volume.

Published 2002 by the Victorian Council of Churches, in
association with the Australian Theological Forum.

Victorian Council of Churches:
306 Little Collins Street, Melbourne, Vic 3000, Australia.
Australian Theological Forum:
PO Box 504, Hindmarsh, SA, 5007, Australia.

ISBN 1 920691 03 0

This book originated with the Social Questions Commission of
the Victorian Council of Churches.

HOW TO GET THE MOST OUT OF THIS BOOK

For Staff of church welfare agencies:

There are two sets of discussion questions: on page 53 at the
end of Paul Oslington s chapter, and on page 87 for more
general discussion about agency values. These questions are
probably appropriate for staff at the level of project manager
and social workers, and above.

We suggest that staff each receive a copy of the book and read
the Oslington chapter before the first session. Then read the
Cleary and Webster responses before the second study. An hour
should be allocated to each session.

For clergy and lay leaders in parishes:

The questions on page 87 are suitable for parishioners involved
in community services. Before discussing the questions
participants need to read the whole book.

Printed by Openbook Print, Adelaide

Contents

145394

The Church and Markets

Brian Howe

'In order to believe in human equality it is necessary to believe in God' (Richard Tawney).

Themes of justice and equality run through the biblical record in both Old and New Testaments. They are implicit in the doctrine of creation, in the *imago dei* doctrine, in the teaching of the prophets and in what Jesus taught about the nature of God and in what the early church taught about Jesus. The struggle to realise these themes was central to the practice of the early church.

> Now the whole group of those who believed were of one heart and soul and no one claimed private ownership of any possessions, but everything they owned was held in common. There was not a needy person among them, for as many who owned lands or houses sold them and brought the proceeds of what was sold. They laid it at the apostles feet and it was distributed to each as had need (Acts 4, 32,34-5).

The themes of justice and liberation from injustice are not the only themes present in the bible but they are certainly compelling themes. They have also been important themes in the history, teaching and practice of the church including in present times such as in the influence of liberation theologians in Latin America, in the civil rights movement in North America, in the struggle to overcome apartheid in Southern Africa or to achieve a democratic constitution in South Korea. However, in societies such as our own there is a sense that whatever the past influence of Christianity in defining our values, our values now rest very much on secular foundations.[1] Even in societies such as the United States in which the place and influence of public religion is widely acknowledged, issues of values and beliefs seem more often than not to be settled on the basis of insights drawn from the social sciences rather than on the basis of religious belief.

When I was a theological student in the mid 1960's in the United States a number of my fellow theological students were interested in ways of understanding and interpreting the Bible in the modern age. Many of these students saw in the social sciences tools which would be important in helping lay people read the New Testament in ways which helped them to over-come the problems of distance between the ancient and the modern world. I have been impressed by the work of Marcus Borg, an American New Testament scholar, who has in his various books[2] certainly helped me to understand both the New Testament and in particular the socio-cultural significance of Jesus in the first century.

Whatever conclusions one may come to about Jesus, it is important to understand the context in which he struggled to reinterpret the historic faith of Judaism while remaining very much within its traditions. We can grasp the shift from essentially a rule based ethic to a more personalistic ethic based on love. But I think Borg's emphasis on the links between this rule ethic and the 'purity system' present in Palestine in the first century enables him to bring out the radical redefinition of human dignity which flowed from Jesus' understanding of the nature of God. God's love was not restricted to those who were free from disease but extended to those whose illness or disease seemed be of the greatest threat to the wellbeing of others. While God's love had been evident in the history of Israel it was in no sense restricted to one race or one people. The ethic which

---

1. Alan Wolff, *Whose Keeper? Social Science and Moral Obligation* (Berkeley: University of California Press, 1989).

2. Marcus Borg, *Jesus in Contemporary Scholarship* (Harrisburgh, Penn: Trinity Press, 1994), *Conflict, Holiness and Politics in the Teaching of Jesus* (Harrisburgh, Penn: Trinity Press, 1998).

Jesus taught was based on a theology which included those that seem to have been excluded under the old order. Of course in challenging this system Jesus also was destroying the authority of those who had a vested interest in its preservation. This undermining of the power structure would inevitably bring him into sharp conflict with those who were benefiting most from the existence of the purity system.

In any society, the values of those who are most wealthy and most powerful tend to be pervasive and thus many of the stories which make up the New Testament reflect this struggle to redefine spirituality in ways which invert this conventional understanding of the sources of power. In the process Jesus begins to build the basis of a new sense of fellowship, which emphasises inclusiveness rather than the barriers which separated people. Borg's interpretation of the story climaxes in the temple where Jesus overturns the tables of money changers and the seats of sellers of sacrificial birds arguing that both the money changers and sellers of birds were part of the temple system which stood at the centre of the tributary mode of production drawing money to the Jerusalem elites.[3] In overturning the tables Jesus was challenging what lay behind the market not the market itself. He was challenging the system of power and privilege which was at the heart of the old order, the old religion. Borg recognised the political nature of this act. However he did not, as a consequence, see Jesus as a politician. His challenge is to a social and political system but it is more than that. It is a challenge to the basis of a religious culture, to a system of beliefs and to all the consequences of adherence to those beliefs and or values.

1. Sen Demonstrates the Importance of Ethics

Oslington notes that basic aspects of contemporary mainstream economics are theologically contentious. While he states that his paper does not provide a theological evaluation of economics, he argues in his conclusion for the inclusion of ethical and theological discussion within economics and within Australian

---

3.   Borg, 1994, 114.

public life. His paper outlines concerns about contracting out within the economic framework itself, but also provides some theological dimensions for consideration in such discussion.

The responses to Oslington's paper from Ray Cleary and Marilyn Webster provide further food for theological reflection on the economic model and its impact on church agencies. The Victorian Council of Churches hopes this publication will promote informed theological debate and discussion within churches and their agencies, about the assumptions underlying economics and contracting out.

Amartya Sen,[4] Nobel prize winning economist and social philosopher, provides a further perspective. Sen has been able to claim attention by questioning the utilitarian assumptions which lie behind so much of the conventional wisdom among economists. Sen thinks that the preoccupation with national income, economic growth, as the most important indicator of human well being has been misguided. It is not that Sen does not see income as being important. Lack of sufficient income is perhaps the most important indicator of poverty. However, income needs to be seen as one means and should not be confused with ends, which are in Sen's view about human development and wellbeing. This is very important in defining the way that we talk about issues such poverty and deprivation. Our concern here is not with providing some minimum income which would enable people to survive at a subsistence level. Rather it is to ensure that people are enabled to participate fully in the life of the community. Sen emphasises the need to see people not as atomised individuals but rather as fulfilling their potential as active members of a community. Poverty then is not about a single indicator but has to do with overcoming the barriers which people may face in realising their potential capability. Failure to achieve potential may reflect lack of income, a poor environment, access to education and or health care. The political system may also prevent people from realising their capabilities by limiting access to power and participation. Sen's emphasis on comprehensive human development does not mean that he does not have a positive view of

---

4.   Sen Amartya, *Development as Freedom* (New York: Alfred A Knopf, 1999).

markets within certain limits. The absence of markets facilitates the concentration of power and influence. Sen does not see the market operating without values and or norms. For a market to operate efficiently there needs to be trust and the use of implicit and explicit norms. However, despite its effectiveness in some areas 'capitalist ethics is deeply limited in some respects and fails to resolve issues of economic inequality, environmental protection and the need for cooperation of different kinds that operate outside of the market'.[5] It is the limitations of markets which is Sen's concern not so much issues to do with the integrity of traders—issues of personal honesty.

Oslington, Cleary and Webster raise other concerns. Oslington expounds the limitations of regulatory economics, even within its own framework. Webster raises concerns from the practice perspective and Cleary raises other questions by looking at the theological underpinning for the work of Christian agencies.

2. The Changing Context
Churches and especially their welfare agencies have recently had their territory defined in terms which blur the distinction between the market economy and civil society. This does raise issues of values and norms, as these agencies historically, for the most part, saw themselves as functioning in ways which were outside of the market system.

Historically, because of the absence of government funded services, churches were motivated by compassion for the poor. This motivation led to the establishment of their many missions and institutions. Along with the sense of the need to serve there was also a commitment to evangelise, to extend the influence of the Christian faith among the people they served. Sometimes this established tensions between the priority given to proselytising the priority given to providing disinterested service.

---

5. Sen, 1999, 263.

During the twentieth century, much of the service and caring that had historically been provided by church-based agencies became the direct responsibility of the state. With this transfer of responsibility, there had also been a secularisation of this care and concern and separation from the traditional theological bases. Increasingly the state funded and influenced the quality of church agency-based services, Some church agencies consciously sought to set new priorities emphasising their role as innovators and pressure groups to persuade government to provide more comprehensive services.

There have also been changes in the values which informed church-based welfare. Whereas in the past the motives of churches and church agencies seem to have been primarily driven by religious and charitable motivations, this seems less true in recent times—not just in welfare but across the spectrum of church–based services and institutions. Many of the wealthiest private schools are owned and managed on behalf of churches and religious societies. Similarly the changing role of hospitals and private health insurance means that many hospitals established by churches and religious societies now serve higher income groups. In the area of welfare services there is less of an emphasis on the very poor and much more emphasis on providing a more professional and well managed service, often designed to take advantage of government funding and to offer career paths for their more professional staff. These services have increasingly been receiving subsidies from governments, which have helped to cover substantial proportions of the costs. Many of the agencies have had charity status and have been eligible for tax subsidies. The subsidies have enabled many agencies to expand their services and to grow in scale. With more assured funding they have been able to employ more professionally qualified staff, undertake more sophisticated corporate planning and often expand the range of the activities and clients served.

The increased scale of activity has been responsible for concerns about accountability with the result that governments in recent years are increasingly looking to adopt new measures to ensure efficiency in the delivery of services as well as the equitable distribution of services. This has included recourse to competitive tendering. The clientele for services has often not reflected the religious origins or sponsorship of agencies. The growing size of agencies has resulted in sometimes quite large numbers of staff, and industrial relations negotiations have become an important part of the life of many church–based agencies. For some agencies the original church base or religious base may no longer exist and agencies may become increasingly distant from their religious roots. The gradual evolution of many of these agencies towards a more secular or professional image and self understanding must be confusing to those who have responsibility for regulating a service which to outsiders may seem as very much a business rather than a charity. It also raises questions for the church too. To what extent are church agencies part of the church in any real sense?

3. Competing with Corporations

As church–based services have been increasingly secularised and often at least partially funded by the state these agencies may find themselves in direct competition with agencies that may have no such religious and charitable foundations and may provide services as businesses whose primary motivation is profit. William Ryan recently visited Australia describing similar trends in the United States. He pointed out there that 'just about everything affecting the provision of social services 'the government agencies that award contracts, the political environment in which they operate, and the preferences of clients has profoundly changed'.[6] Major secular corporations are just as likely to be offering health, education or welfare services. Ryan draws attention to the danger that this competition may present to non-profits especially the danger to the core values or motivations which have been important where the profit motivation has not been a major driver. The issue, William Ryan argues, is not so much whether these agencies can survive facing the competition of profit-oriented businesses. 'The real issue is whether non-profits can adapt

---

6. William Ryan, 'The New Landscape for Non Profits' in *Harvard Business Review*, January/February 1999: 128.

without compromising the qualities that distinguish them from profit organizations'.[7] This shift is occurring according to Ryan partly because of the shift on the part of government to outsourcing services, a consequence of the push for smaller government. It is also occurring because business is increasingly being seen as a good role model for delivering quality services efficiently. Both Oslington and Webster reflect this issue in different ways.

In this volume, Paul Oslington, within the framework of his discipline as an economist, reflects on why church agencies are seeking to undertake more and more government contracting in the welfare area and why governments are so keen to have them there. Oslington suggests that governments want lower costs, and the higher quality of services which committed agencies can deliver, and they want to access the accumulated experience and infra-structure, an altruistic workforce, the donated dollar and the trust which welfare agencies have often built up over the years. These agencies and their staff and support base, together with the related networks, represent social capital which governments are able to access. On the other hand churches access finance, earn status, buy some influence and perhaps most significantly can grow in scale. Indeed, as Oslington points out, along with scale there are increased financial risks.

Oslington reflects on some of the dilemmas which non-government or church-based agencies face in contracting with governments to provide specific services such as employment services. His greatest concern is the 'monopsony power' of the bureaucracy as the single purchaser of services having very different objectives to the agencies which are contracted to provide, say, employment services. The concern of the bureaucracy may be primarily about throughput. The concern of the agency may be primarily about the quality of the service provided. The reality is that markets rarely operate as they are intended to do in theory and need to be regulated or supplemented in various ways. In today's labour market there is an

---

7.   Ryan, 1999, 128.

ever higher premium placed on skill. Those with lesser skills are being increasingly pushed to the margins of the labour market and experiencing unemployment or under employment.

Church agencies may see a need for a much greater investment in education and training which from the point of view of the government may result in less throughput and too high costs. The problem with markets is that they reflect inequality, as Sen observes, and they do not address or redress inequality. In part the participation of church–based agencies in providing employment services reflects a sense of compassion or charity but in so far as it does not address the heart of the problem, say the need to sub-stantially upgrade the skills of the unemployed and the under employed, it does not reflect the commitment of churches to equality and social justice. It may also compromise church agencies by increasingly involving them in cost saving measures such as 'breaching' which has pushed large numbers of income security recipients into poverty.[8] In this case the church is allowing itself and its agencies to be coopted into a system which is much more about blaming the victim than finding a solution to the serious problems of unemployment and under employment.

4. Conclusion
In this publication the Victorian Council of Churches wants to draw attention to the increasing tendency of churches and church agencies to become more market oriented as they accept more opportunities to contract with the state on a commercial or quasi-commercial basis. There are issues here about the distribution of risk in the contracts that are signed and the extent to which these agencies are in fact becoming uncritical agencies of the state as opposed to providing disinterested (or independent?) services. Oslington fairly and objectively asks these questions as an economist while offering some theological observations. Some agencies such as Good Shepherd are scrupulous in ensuring that any contracts they sign are in line

---

8.   Australian Council of Social Service, *Doling out Punishment, the Rise and Rise of Social Security Breaches* (Sydney: ACOSS, 2000).

with their mission, formulating a code which would ensure that in their work with families and young people they would seek to maintain the integrity of their developmental approach. There are issues here of the integrity of the third sector and its capacity to maintain its independence from government as opposed to the legitimate need for government to ensure accountability when it contracts with agencies to undertake work on its behalf. In some areas, particularly in corrections, this line is still being negotiated. Key words such as partnership are being negotiated as to whether they provide the right definition of the relationship between government and the non-government or third sector.

Webster, in her response to Oslington, takes up related themes and identifies the pressures of contracting out on the mission of agencies and on the quality of the workforce in terms of commitment to mission. She notes the pressure on agencies to focus on government defined priorities, sometimes at the expense of the human need they are confronted with through their clients. She also identifies threats to a Christian holistic approach to client need, and to agencies committed to community and to work for justice.

The most important concerns of the churches should not be restricted to the internal integrity of markets but should go to the limitations of markets in building a fair or just society. However, this is not to minimise the issues raised by Oslington which require churches to look, as should any business, at the full implications of pursuing a particular contract. Does meeting the conditions of this contract really advance the mission or purposes of the church agency or business, not only in the short term but in the longer term as well? There are also broader concerns about the role of the church in society to face the tension between its commitment as a community of responsible citizens and its commitment to a more radical transformation of society. The market tends to reflect the existing distribution of income and power, thus favouring those who have most resources.

To return to our beginning: at the heart of the Christian faith is our belief in equality. Not just equality of opportunity but the equality which we all have before God. Indeed Richard Tawney went so far as to say, 'In order to believe in human equality it is necessary to believe in God. It is only when one contemplates the infinitely great that human differences appear infinitely small as to be negligible'.[9] Of course Tawney's concept on equality was sophisticated He saw equality as fundamentally linked to liberty as a condition of freedom. Tawney argued:

> A large measure of equality, so far from being inimical to liberty is essential to it. Liberty is in fact equality in action, in the sense that not all men perform identical functions or wield the same degree of power, but that all men are equally protected against the basis of power, and equally entitled to insist that power should be used, not for personal ends, but for the general advantage.[10]

There is a contemporary parallel here in the writing of Sen especially in his *Development as Freedom*. He sees justice not as a means of increasing individual utility or as sharing a limited number of goods in a fair manner, but rather as realising the capacity of people to fully participate in the life of the community. There needs to be a transformation of society in which people's equality as citizens is recognised in our commitment to human development. As important as it may be to build human capital to invest in people and enhance their capability as the demands of creating wealth, it is even more important to build social capital—ie strengthen the relationships between people so that they form a stronger community. Having said that, there are yet other dimensions which Tawney described as the spiritual

---

9. Quoted in Duncan B Forrester, *On Human Worth*, 2001, 139

10. Forrester, D B on Human Worth (SCM Press: London, 2001), 33.

Possibilities for human life are often not realised because people are diverted to worship the false Gods, which are so distracting. People's worship of wealth and power has the force of a cult which has strange antics of devotion, and singular observances, and a ritual sometimes comic, sometimes cruel, sometimes both. It causes its devotee to admire what is not admirable, while despising what is, and to go seek happiness where it cannot be found, not where it can. It is not favourable to simplicity of life for it makes much of display; to sincerity of mind for it burns incense to shams; or to a just and sensitive taste, for its criteria are quantity and mass.[11]

It is important to emphasise the need for greater equality in the distribution of wealth Tawney argues, not so much because wealth is the most important thing in life but to prove that it is not. The paradox of poverty amidst unprecedented affluence is a paradox which Tawney felt required a theological, a spiritual answer. In a world which is increasingly polarised between those who use more than their fair share of the world's resources and those have too small a share, Tawney's words still resonate. There have recently been more people suggesting that rising inequality is either a fiction or does not matter. Christians must strongly resist such suggestions. A belief in equality is at the heart of our faith as Christians. It should be at the core of our practice of discipleship.

---

11.   Tawney, R H, *Equality* (Harcourt Bruce & Company: New York, 1931), 272.

Economic and Theological Issues in Contracting out of Welfare and Labour Market Services

Paul Oslington

This research has been commissioned by the Victorian Council of Churches Commission on Social Questions, and coordinated by Professor Brian Howe of the Centre for Public Policy, University of Melbourne. I had reservations about undertaking the project as I have worked in the past on more general issues in the relationship between economics and theology, and my first hand knowledge of the welfare sector is fairly limited. Nevertheless I appreciate the opportunity to write on this important topic and have learnt much over the past few months. It must be emphasised that this project is undertaken in a private capacity and the views expressed should not be attributed to the University of New South Wales or the Australian Defence Force Academy.

The paper has been written for church people concerned about the issues, for those working in the welfare sector and for policy makers. The paper is fairly informal, although references to the technical economics and theology literatures are given in the guide to further reading. A paper with an economic model formalising some of the arguments of the report is in progress. I hope that the paper will stimulate some new thinking about the issue of contracting–out of welfare and labour market services and lead to improvements in the arrangements if they are to continue.

1. Background

In a period where the state dominates the provision of welfare, it is worth remembering that it has not always been so. Churches pioneered welfare as we know it and state provision was stimulated by, and modelled on, work the religious organisations were already doing. Gradually through the twentieth century, state provision became more important, with important landmarks being the response to mass unemployment in the 1930s, the introduction of state pensions in the 1940s, changing family patterns in the 1960s, and the dramatic rise in unemployment in the 1970s. Through the 1980s there was widespread questioning of the welfare state driven by concerns about expenditure levels, demographic predictions of further rises in expenditure and declines in the number of tax paying workers, the lack of success in reducing unemployment rates, and concerns that certain groups were becoming trapped in a cycle of dependence on welfare.

Over the past few years a series of reforms in the US have dismantled the centralised welfare system to the extent that work (often at very low wages), private charity, starvation or crime are the only options available. Incentives to work are at the centre of the US reforms, coming from a view that only through work can the poor truly be helped. The charitable choice provisions of the US reforms have meant that community groups and churches are increasingly important as providers of remaining welfare. These trends are likely to continue under the current administration, perhaps with an even greater emphasis on church organisations as providers. While there has been some success in moving people in the US from welfare to work, the last ten years have been a period of remarkably strong growth and it remains to be seen how the 'reformed' welfare system copes with the inevitable economic downturn. In the UK there have been similar calls and some changes, but the current government is cautious about going further down the US road.

In Australia our welfare system has become more targeted, with increasingly specific eligibility requirements. Unemployment benefits have become harder to get, and more is required of recipients. As in the US, there has also been a move towards churches and community organisations as providers of welfare. The most dramatic example of this has been the recent abolition of the government employment agency and the contracting–out of almost all labour market matching and training services, with church organisations winning a significant proportion of the contracts. Interestingly the rhetoric of reform in Australia has moved away from an early concern with reducing costs to follow the US in emphasising the moral benefits of winding back the welfare state.

2. Why Church Agencies are Attractive to the Government as Deliverers of Services

Before undertaking the evaluation of contracting–out it is worth trying to understand why the government finds it attractive. The first part of this question is why contracting–out might be preferred by the government to direct provision, and the second why the church welfare organisations rather than for-profit firms might be attractive to the government. Some reasons for preferring contracting are:

2.1 Lower costs. The evidence so far on contracting–out of welfare and labour market services, in particular job matching and training, is that there have been substantial cost savings for the government. Why might this be so? The most commonly heard argument for contracting–out is that the competitive discipline of the market increases efficiency and lowers costs. In recent Australian public policy discussion competition has been presented as a magic cure for all manner of ills, real and imagined. However, the meaning of competition in recent Australian public policy discussion is not necessarily the same as in mainstream economic theory, nor do many of the statements made have much foundation in economic theory. Economists would wish to look behind the invocation of competition to see where the cost savings are actually coming from.

One possibility is that the organisations which win the contracts are able to pay lower wages than the government. This might be because government employees are unionised and are in a stronger bargaining position than employees of the contractor. Government employees find it easier to organise and may be able to negotiate with an employer subject to all sorts of political constraints. Apart from these inherent differences between the bargaining position of workers in the two types of organisations, the move to contracting turns over staff forcing new contracts to be written. If lower wages are the source of the costs savings from contracting–out, then it is important to recognise from an economic point of view that this is not an efficiency gain, but rather a transfer from workers in the industry to the government. Another possibility might be that that wages remain the same but the intensity of work increases, but again this would be a transfer from workers to the government rather than a real efficiency gain.

Another reason for cost savings might be that there are stronger incentives for private sector organisations to reorganise operations to eliminate waste, and to innovate in ways which reduce costs. It is certainly true that under contracting cost savings accrue to the organisation which has won the contract, but the important thing is whether the incentives for the organisation are reflected in incentives for the workers. If there are strong incentives for workers to eliminate waste and innovate, then contracting–out can improve efficiency compared to a government organisations where incentives for workers to eliminate waste and innovate have traditionally been weak.

However, if the crucial issue is incentives workers face, then it would not seem impossible for government organisations to replicate the incentives for waste reduction and innovation that private firms offer, and so reap the efficiency gains associated with contracting–out.

2.2 Quality. In the Australian debate over contracting–out of welfare and labour market services, the higher quality service provided by non-government organisations has been an important part of the argument for contracting–out. This contrasts with the debate over contracting out in other areas like cleaning services, where it is recognised that quality is harmed and where a decision on contracting–out depends on the tradeoff between quality reductions and cost savings.

The evidence suggests that non-government organisations are better providers of welfare and labour market services but it is difficult to argue that this is a result of contracting–out. After all contracting–out is very recent. It would seem to have more to do with the nature of the not-for-profit and church organisations, and the important quality question is the impact of contracting–out on quality of service provided by these sorts of organisations. This will be considered in the evaluation section of the report.

2.3 Politics. Contracting–out might be attractive to the government because it shifts responsibility for social ills like unemployment to other organisations. Even if under contracting the ultimate legal responsibility remains with the government, the fact that non-government organisations are actually delivering the services greatly affects the public's perception of responsibility. A related issue is the way contracting reduces the ability of welfare recipients and others to appeal and seek redress against welfare decisions, as the services are not being delivered by the government and administrative law does not apply in the same way. Information is also more difficult to obtain about the functioning of the welfare system in a contracting environment. Furthermore, offering government contracts can be a way of co-opting non-government organisations and reducing criticism of government policies. The inclusion of confidentiality clauses in contracts and restrictions on public comment suggests this is important for the government.

These reasons of reducing costs, improved quality and politics apply to contracting–out regardless of the organisations that win the contracts, but there are some additional reasons why contracting to not-for-profit organisations, and more specifically to church organisations might be attractive to the government.

2.4 Accumulated experience and infrastructure. Not-for-profit and church organisations have been providing welfare services for longer than governments and have built up expertise, as well as contacts and trust. Governments can draw on these accumulated advantages through the contracting process.

2.5 Altruistic workforces. Not-for-profit and church organisations tend to attract altruistic and highly motivated individuals. This tendency has some basis in economic theory as a rational altruist has an incentive to choose these organisations because the constitutional prohibition against distributing profits provides some assurance that the fruits of their altruism will not be appropriated by shareholders, as they would tend to be in a for-profit firm.

2.6 Donors. Church organisations benefit from substantial past and current donations, and to the extent that these do not dry up when they take government contracts, the cost and quality benefits provided by donations can to some extent be exploited by the government. Even if current donations dry up, past donations are still exploitable through contracting. Note that the rational donor will have the similar preference for a not-for-profit firm as a rational altruistic worker, but that this preference will be stronger the greater the constitutional protection against the future exploitation of their donations.

2.7 Client trust. In an environment where clients of an organisation have imperfect information about quality of service provided by different organisation, not-for-profit status can act as a signal of quality. The client will see that not-for-profit status weakens the incentives for the organisation to trade off quality for cost savings which boost distributable profits, and so will tend to rationally choose and trust not-for-profit organisations. Again, the government can take advantage of this through the contracting process, to the extent that taking contracts does not destroy it.

2.8 Participation. If participation by clients in the organisation is a good thing, and leads to better outcomes, then contracting may be attractive to the government as a way of facilitating this. The nature of government organisations precludes this sort of participation, and contracting with participatory not-for-profit organisations can thus be efficiency-enhancing.

All of the above are reasons why the government might find contracting–out of welfare and labour market services to church

organisations attractive, and help explain the move to contracting. The next two sections evaluate contracting out from
the points of view of economics and theology.

3. Economic Concerns about Contracting–Out

Before commencing an economic evaluation of contracting–out
it important to understand a little about the nature of
contemporary mainstream economics. Economics looks at the
efficiency of arrangements—whether arrangements maximise
social welfare. For a contemporary mainstream economist social
welfare means welfare of the individuals who make up a
society, where individual welfare depends on the satisfaction of
individual preferences. (Note that welfare here means some-
thing quite different to when we speak of welfare services or
the welfare sector). Measuring social welfare is quite difficult,
and in practice economists advocate arrangements which
maximise national income or Gross Domestic Product (GDP).
There are well known problems with GDP as a measure of
welfare, for instance as, many things which contribute to
individual welfare are not traded in markets and thus not
counted.

It is worth highlighting some aspects of the approach of
contemporary mainstream economics. Firstly, in the language
of moral philosophy, it is consequentialist. Actions, including
changes in regulatory arrangements, are evaluated solely on
their consequences. Nothing is intrinsically good or right.
Secondly, the approach is highly individualist. Social welfare is
the welfare of individuals; things are only good for society if
individuals value them. Thirdly, each individual is the judge of
his or her own welfare and their valuations are not subject to
any outside standard. All of these aspects of the practice of
economists are theologically contentious, but this is not the
place for a full theological evaluation of economics. In the
evaluation of contracting-out that follows, the tools of
economics will be used with little further comment. This
concedes much, but if contracting-out can be shown to be
problematic within the framework which is commonly used to
justify it, this should be cause for concern.

The particular branch of economics that is relevant to contracting-out is regulatory economics, which is about designing regulatory arrangements that maximise the social welfare or GDP. It has been used in Australia in recent times to redesign arrangements for electricity, telecommunications, and other industries. Regulatory economics is a difficult and subtle branch of economics, and much of the difficulty comes from the existence of market power, transaction costs, strategic interactions between powerful participants, and imperfect information for both those in the industry and the regulator.

A framework which is often used to assess regulatory arrangements is the principal-agent model. Think about selling a house. You, the owner, act as principal in contracting with an agent to sell your house, but there is a problem of getting the agent to act in your interests when you cannot observe the actions of agent. Continuous supervision of the agent would be imperfect, costly and seem to defeat the purpose of the agency relationship. As an alternative to supervision, the principal would like to design a contract which aligns the incentives of the real estate agent with those of the principal eg to maximise the sale price.

This idea can be transferred to the relationship between the government and the organisations with which it contracts. The government is the principal trying to design a contract which provides incentives for the welfare agencies to act in the interests of the government. The role of the regulatory economist is to assist in designing contracts which are efficient in the sense of maximising social welfare. In some regulatory economics the government is assumed to have the interests of society at heart, but sometimes a more sophisticated analysis is used which considers divergences between government objectives and social welfare. The principal-agent structure of contracting-out of labour market services is illustrated in the figure 1.

Figure 1 - Principal-Agent Structure

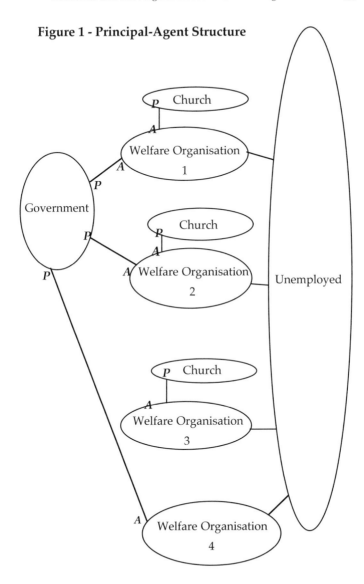

In figure 1 the government as principal (P) is contracting with agents (A) welfare organisations 1,2 and 3 to provide labour market services to the unemployed. Welfare organisation 3 does not contract with the government and provides labour market services funded in other ways. Note that welfare organisations 1,2 and 3 are church organisations, and are in a principal-agent relationship with the churches as well as the government. Welfare organisation 4 is a secular not-for-profit organisation, or perhaps a for-profit organisation that has entered the welfare industry as a result of contracting-out.

The task is to evaluate the contracting arrangements between the government and the welfare organisations. So as to be able to be more specific about contracting arrangements, I will focus on the Job Network contract documents, although many of the issues are common to other welfare and labour market contracts. From the point of view of regulatory economics there are a number of problems with the Job Network contracts. These are:

3.1 Incentives to erode quality of service
Quality of service, in contrast to cost, is often difficult to observe and even if it can be observed, difficult for a third party to verify. If quality is not verifiable, then enforceable contracts cannot be written for it. In situations where quality of service is important to the principal, the contract must be structured carefully so that the agent has an incentive to provide quality, or at least does not have strong incentives to erode it.

One of the lessons of regulatory economics is that where quality is unverifiable and important to the principal, fixed price contracts are inappropriate and some form of cost plus contractual payment works better. The reason is that fixed price contracts provide powerful incentives to reduce costs as cost savings accrue to the contractor, and one obvious way of reducing costs is to erode quality of service. With the alternative cost reimbursement contract, these strong incentives to reduce quality do not exist.

For welfare and labour market services quality is surely important, and as the main dimensions of quality are difficult to verify, cost plus contracts are more appropriate. However, the existing Job Network contracts are fixed price, indicating either ignorance by the designers of the contracting arrangements of basic principles of regulatory economics or else a strong preference for cost reduction over quality of service. If the latter, then the design of the contracts is sharply inconsistent with the emphasis in government policy documents on using contracting to improve the quality of labour market services.

Some additional comments are necessary about the discussion of quality in some of the Job Network documents. Firstly, there is much discussion of the importance of quality in decisions about the organisations to which contracts are awarded. However, it seems that what is meant by quality here is successful outcomes (eg placement rates) so that it is really quantity of services delivered that is being referred to rather than quality of service. The most important dimensions of quality are unverifiable, even if observable by participants. Secondly, in the documentation it is argued that quality is protected by having a minimum price for certain labour market services. Such a minimum price will only make a difference if it is set high enough to be binding, but if it is set at this level then it will undermine the tendering process because tenderers will have no incentive to bid above this price. It is thus difficult to take the minimum price seriously. More importantly though, the argument about a minimum price guaranteeing quality misses the basic regulatory economics point that it is the fixing of the price that creates the incentives to erode unverifiable quality, irrespective of the level it is fixed at.

Overall if quality is important, then a move towards cost plus-reimbursement contract would improve efficiency, with the exact position on the cost reimbursement vs fixed price spectrum being determined by society's tradeoff between quality and cost savings in Job Network Services.

3.2 *Multiple agency*

Welfare agencies which take on government contracts, as has been noted, are in a principal/agent relationship both with the government and their parent church or other organisations. This has important implications for the types of incentives the government should offer because the overall incentives for the agency workers depend on the interaction between the incentives offered by both principals. The regulatory economics literature suggests where there is a multiple agency relationship the incentives offered by both principals should be fairly low powered, tending towards cost reimbursement rather than fixed price.

For the agencies, conflicts between the incentives provided by the government and church principals may be an important part of the confusion of mission felt within an organisation. These conflicts may increase as the churches associated with some of the agencies seek to exert greater control over the agencies to counteract the effects of contracting on the organisations.

3.3 *Reduced incentives for collaboration between agencies*

Collaboration between agencies can bring many benefits. Coordinated action, exchange of information, and learning from other agencies innovations can reduce costs and improve quality of service.

Another of the lessons of regulatory economics is that where collaboration is beneficial, some sort of reward for joint output improves efficiency. The current Job Network contracts however reward agencies only for their own output and do not provide incentives for collaboration. The disincentives to collaborate are reinforced by the newness of the contracting-out of Job Network services which means agencies are inevitably evaluated against other agencies' performance rather than some historical or international standard—this means agencies' own measured performance can be improved by undermining the performance of other agencies.

Consideration should be given to some form of joint reward for the performance of all agencies, and if joint rewards are impractical then the incentives for individual agencies should be lower powered.

3.4 *Competition in the long-term*
In assessing the cost and quality effects of contracting-out it is important to take a long-term view. There are many cases of contracting-out yielding initial cost savings but costs being higher in the long term because as particular contractors gain a dominant position in the market, they are able to push up prices and reduce quality. This has been a particular problem in rural areas where there is only a limited number of potential tenderers.

One of the consequences of contracting-out has been to reduce the number of welfare agencies, especially driving out smaller agencies. This has happened despite provisions in the tendering process which prevent a single agency winning all the work in a particular location. While a reduction in the number of agencies pushing up prices may not be so much of a problem for the Job Network (at least in metropolitan areas) there is cause for concern over the loss of the distinctive high quality services and innovation which comes so often from the smaller agencies.

More thought should be given in the contracting process to ways of supporting smaller agencies that provide high quality or innovative services.

3.5 *Costs of tendering and compliance*
One of the problems of the Job Network, which has been acknowledged in the recent documentation, is the high costs of the tendering process both for the Department and the agencies. These tendering costs waste resources and undermine any other efficiency gains there might be from contracting-out. As well as wasting resources, the high costs of tendering reduce the number of tenders, potentially increasing costs and reducing quality.

The costs of complying with additional government requirements that go with contracting (eg regular reporting, more
sophisticated financial systems) have not received as much
attention in the recent documentation, but are economically
very similar to tendering costs, wasting resources and reducing
the number of tenderers.

There are no easy solutions to this problem, but more
thought needs to be given to ways of reducing these costs for
the agencies.

3.6 Professionalisation and careerism of agencies

A recent theme of regulatory economics has been the indirect
effects of professionalisation and career concerns. This comes
from the idea that workers are motivated not just by current
rewards but by future career prospects. To gain these future
career rewards workers try to influence their perceived value to
potential employers by altering their effort level and the
allocation of effort over different tasks associated with their job.
These career concerns are particularly important in government
and not-for-profit agencies because current rewards are often
weak compared to those in for-profit firms.

Contracting-out of welfare and labour market services has
led to professionalisation of agency workforces because there
are many new tasks which require special expertise and the
financial stakes are higher. This has greatly affected the culture
of the agencies, about which some strong views have been
expressed. From the point of view of economic theory, these
career concern effects induced by contracting-out can be
positive or negative. For instance, if agencies cannot observe
each others' costs but quality of service is observable (without
necessarily being verifiable) then workers best enhance their
perceived value to other agencies by concentrating on
providing quality services. This may counterbalance the
incentives to cut down quality that have already been noted to
be a consequence of fixed price contracts for Job Network
Services. Another benefit of career structures induced by
contracting-out may be higher incentives effort, but possible
gains must here balanced against the erosion of the altruism

that is so important in these organisations. On the negative side, career concerns may lead to the diversion of effort to unproductive activities eg spending agency resources on enhancing worker's personal profiles, organising and attending pointless conferences to cultivate relationships with potential employers.

In my view the changes in career incentives and organisational culture and the changes that come with contracting-out are extremely important, but they are complex and more work needs to be done within the welfare agencies and by regulators to understand and deal with them.

3.7 *Loss of advocacy*

The role of advocacy in achieving efficient outcomes has received attention in the recent regulatory economics literature. Competition among advocates can generate valuable information for decision makers, improve incentives for decision makers by providing external checks of actions, and also ensure that preferences of dispersed groups are not ignored in the political process. For these reasons governments can improve efficiency in certain circumstances by creating advocates, such as when they fund prosecutors and defence counsel in an adversarial legal system.

Welfare and labour market policy would seem to be an area where the agencies have information from their first hand experience of dealing with recipients which is valuable to the government and where there is a dispersed group which would not otherwise have a voice in the political process.

Much controversy has been generated by confidentiality provisions of recent welfare and labour market contracts and restrictions on commenting on government policy. There is also a tendency to sharply separate service delivery from advocacy so that government funds are not used for advocacy. In the light of the recent regulatory economics, these provisions may be efficiency reducing, and there are arguments for the government encouraging and funding advocacy. This is of course only true if the government is truly concerned about efficiency, not about using contracting to manipulating political debate about welfare and labour market in unhealthy ways.

3.8 Risk compensation

Under the Job Network contracts almost all risk is carried by the contractor. Consider risk associated with changes in economic conditions. Job Network tenders must prepare bids well before the contract period begins, then contracts last for three years. Over this period economics conditions can change, and these changes affect the size of the pool of unemployed workers and the ease of placing them in jobs. During a recession there are more potential clients, but finding them jobs becomes more difficult and costly for the agency. While agencies can attempt to forecast economic conditions, professional economists' forecasting record is patchy at best and the agencies cannot be reasonably expected to eliminate this type of risk. The situation is made worse because government action influences economic conditions, so one party to the contract can act in ways which increase costs for the other party, with no contractual compensation. As well as influencing economic conditions the government's labour market and training policies can influence the profitability of Job Network services. For instance a substantial increase in the number of training places would draw potential clients, especially easier to place clients, increasing the average difficulty and cost of the agency placing clients in jobs.

This risk issue is probably one mainly for the agencies, to ensure their tender prices include sufficient compensation for bearing risk, or to negotiate contract clauses which allow prices to be adjusted when economic conditions change or government policy changes in ways which affect agency costs. Another possibility for the agencies is to take on a portfolio of contracts that minimise risk eg contracting for some services for which are more costly during recessions and others which are less costly, although it is recognised that there will be far fewer of the latter. Uncompensated risk is an issue for the government to the extent that it reduces the number of tenders, especially by more prudent and responsible agencies.

3.9 *Monopsony power*

Just as a single seller of a product (a monopolist) can raise prices by restricting output leading to an economically inefficient outcome, so a single purchaser of a service (a monopsonist) can restrict the quantity purchased and drive the price down leading to an economically inefficient outcome. Consider figure 2 which shows the price and quantity of a service. Assume that marginal benefit (i.e. the benefit of the last unit purchased) of the service declines as more of the service is purchased. Assume that costs of providing the service increase as more is provided, perhaps because providers vary in their efficiency and less efficient providers enter the market as quantity increases. In figure 2 a profit maximising monopsonist will choose the quantity Q^M which equates marginal cost with marginal benefit, and pay price P^M which is less than marginal cost for the service. By contrast if there were many purchasers of the service operating in a competitive market, the quantity purchased would be Q^C and price P^C paid. Associated with the higher price and lower quantity there is a measurable efficiency loss, or national income loss from monopsony.

Figure 2 - Analysis of Monopsony

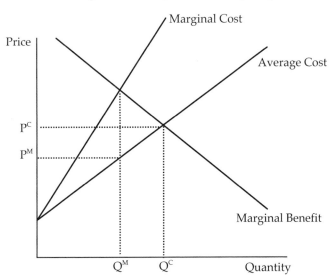

This analysis of monopsony applies as much to the government purchaser as the sole purchaser of Job Network services as it does to a sole private purchaser. Budget surplus maximisation by the Department (where the budget surplus equals the benefits of the services provided less contracted costs) will result in an inefficiently low quantity of Job Network services being purchased at inefficiently low prices. There would thus be efficiency gains in the government increasing quantities and prices relative to those which would be chosen by bureaucrats focusing on the departmental budget.

3.10 Imperfect regulators

The analysis of regulation has so far assumed the government is a single unit which chooses regulatory arrangements to maximise social welfare. While this is a convenient simplification for many purposes, it does not capture the realities of government. In reality the government is a collection of individual politicians and bureaucrats, each with there own interests. Incentive problems within government may be at least as severe as those in the interaction of the government with the welfare agencies, and some of these which arise in the contracting-out of welfare and labour market services will now be considered.

The first problem is conflicts between politicians interested in re-election and the interests of society. This is a principal agent problem where the voters are principals and the politicians agents. Ideally the electoral system should be designed to minimise these conflicts but in reality many conflicts of interest remain. For example, politicians can use the power to influence the allocation of contracts to buy political favours or silence critics.

The second problem is that even if the politicians are unconcerned about re-election and act to maximise social welfare, there would still be a problem aligning the interests of the bureaucrats who implement policy with the interests of society. This is a principal agent problem where the politicians are principals and the bureaucrats are agents. For bureaucrats, department budgets are typically the focus, as they determine rewards, both monetary and non-monetary. In some cases bureaucrats will expand their budgets beyond the socially optimal level, while in other situations the incentives will be to cut costs in budgets at the expense of other things which are valued by society. In the case of welfare and labour market contracting–out it would seem that the incentives to cut costs dominate, especially to cut short–term costs. Cutting short–term costs is a verifiable basis for a bonus or promotion, while unverifiable quality of service is irrelevant in a public service reward system where only verifiable outcomes count. It is this kind of incentive problem which is behind the abuse of monopsony power considered above. The same sort of arguments for giving contractors low-powered incentives in situations where quality matters apply to giving public servants low-powered incentives to reduce costs. Fixed wages and a low emphasis on cost savings in promotion criteria are appropriate where quality of service is important.

As well as the problem of perverse incentives to cut costs, there are also issues about the composition of the costs. Bureaucrats have an incentive to favour methods which increase the value of their own skills. For instance, those with managerial expertise have an incentive to choose methods which are managerial labour-intensive rather than intensive in the use of other types of labour. Replacing in-house provision of welfare services with a contractor reduces the usage and value of welfare worker labour, while increasing the value of legal and managerial labour needed in the tender and contract management process.

To summarise this section; there are substantial problems from the point of view of regulatory economics with the way the Job Network and similar welfare and labour market contracting out has been conducted. It is therefore likely that these problems will erode the capacity of the agencies to provide the high-quality low-cost services which the government finds so attractive at the moment.

In conducting this evaluation, the question has been; how many of the criticisms of the contracting process made by the welfare agencies are supported by modern regulatory economics? The dispute over contracting-out should not be seen as between economics and soft headed welfare workers, but rather between the simplistic and sometimes self-serving rhetoric of contracting-out and a more sophisticated economic analysis which properly considers imperfect information and incentive issues.

4. Theological Concerns about Contracting-Out
The evaluation of contracting out in the last section was from the perspective of contemporary mainstream economic theory, which, as has been pointed out, is not theologically neutral, nor completely separable from theology. Historical and philo-sophical relationships between theology and economics are explored in the guide to further reading.

As well as the theological adequacy of economic theory, three issues are central to an assessment of contracting-out of welfare and labour market services to church organisations: the theol-ogy of markets, the theology of the state, and the nature and mission of the church. Each of these will be considered in turn.

4.1 Theological evaluation of markets
Markets are one way of organising society, and a way that has been increasingly used in Australia in recent years. In evaluating markets it is important to recognise that the market is an institution—a particular set of behaviours—not an object apart from the individuals who behave in these particular ways.

Mainstream economists like markets because they allocate resources efficiently. It can be shown that under certain assumptions (eg perfect competition, complete markets for all commodities, absence of externalities and public goods) a market economy maximises national income for given national resources.

Theologians have held a wide range of views about markets. When economics took shape as a discipline in the eighteenth and early nineteenth century Britain, most theologians took a positive view of markets. Some, like William Paley, TR Malthus, Richard Whately and Thomas Chalmers, made important theoretical contributions to the new discipline and used the insights of economics about market order in their arguments for the existence and goodness of God. For these writers the market was a God-given instrument for the preservation of society and the wonders of market order were proof of God's providential care for humanity. Later in the nineteenth century and into the twentieth century, opinion turned against markets—exemplified by F D Maurice, R H Tawney and William Temple. For these writers, markets were inconsistent with Christian theology as they were driven by greed, and fed inequality and other ills. Socialism was much preferred. A recent writer in this tradition, the British Anglican theologian John Milbank, describes economics as a heretical theodicy.[1] Over the past twenty years there has been a move in the opposite direction, exemplified by the American Catholic theologian Michael Novak and a group of Anglicans associated with Thatcherism in Britain. These recent writers have tended not to emphasise the efficiency properties of markets that attract economists, but the moral benefits of markets such as promoting freedom, rewarding work, and providing outlets for human creativity. It is probably fair to say that despite recent moves, the majority of church people, especially those commenting on public policy and involved in welfare work, are quite negative about markets.

A theological evaluation of markets matters because contracting-out of welfare services is an extension of the domain of markets. We in the churches need to think carefully and theologically about markets, moving beyond our inherited assumptions about markets—whether they be positive or negative. It is important also not to uncritically accept the

---

1.   A theodicy is a philosophical attempt to vindicate the justice and goodness of
      God, in view of the fact of evil.

criteria for evaluating markets that economics offers, with its implicit individualism and consequentialism.

4.2 Evaluation of the state

Economics is ambivalent in its evaluation of the state. One strand of economics sees the state acting ins the interests of society, intervening to correct market failure, redistributing income, and contributing to social welfare in other ways. Another strand of the literature sees the state instead as made up of self-interested individual politicians and bureaucrats, and suggests that the actions of these individuals are unlikely to be in the interests of society. This strand suggests government failure is at least as much of a problem as market failure.

Different theologians evaluate the state in quite divergent ways. Following Augustine, many see the state as a God-given instrument for restraining evil in a fallen world. Others fear the concentration of power and consequent potential for evil that the state represents. Others see the state as meddling with the God-ordained natural order—a view which complements the evaluation of markets as a God-given instrument. For others the state usurps the place that belongs to God—it becomes a counterfeit god that society looks to cure all problems. In Catholic social thought the doctrine of subsidiarity attempts to limit the responsibility of the state and stop it becoming a false god in this way. Subsidiarity restricts the state to functions that cannot be performed by lower level organisations, such as firms and community groups. A similar idea is expressed by the Calvinist doctrine of 'Sphere sovereignty'.

Attitudes to the state are crucial to an evaluation of contracting-out. In one sense contracting-out is a contraction or reduction of the domain of the state, although the state still controls the contracting process and determines what is to be rewarded. To the extent that previously autonomous welfare organisations are brought under the control of the state, contracting-out may be seen as an expansion of state control. Whether we evaluate the expansion of the domain of the state flowing from contracting positively or negatively depends very much on our underlying theology of the state.

4.3 Nature and mission of the church

The theological question here is how the church welfare agencies relate to the church and its mission. To put the question more sharply: what would be the theological consequences of the agencies becoming secularised service deliverers heavily reliant on government contracts? This is the direction contracting out seems to be pushing the church welfare agencies.

If welfare agencies are considered part of the church, then for their transformation into secularised service deliverers to be a bad thing it must be able to be shown that the work they do is theologically important and also that this work should be carried out within the church rather than outside it. On the first issue, it is difficult to resist the theological arguments from creation and the incarnation, that God cares about human suffering and that we should be working to alleviate it. Those who reject this typically do so on the basis of a theologically dubious dichotomy between spiritual and physical needs. The second issue of how exactly our responsibility to alleviate suffering should be put into practice is more difficult. Some would argue that in a liberal democracy, individual Christians should work through the state, or through voluntary organisations not necessarily associated with the church, to alleviate suffering and fight against causes of suffering. Others see the church as the appropriate body through which Christians should work towards the alleviation of suffering and its causes.

In sorting through this issue we need to consider different views of the nature and mission of the church. The American Roman Catholic theologian Avery Dulles suggests five main models of the church, and each will now be described and their implications for contracting-out of welfare services considered.

a) The church as institution:

This model finds classic expression of the Catholic Counter-Reformation writer Robert Bellarmine: 'The one and true Church is the community of men brought together by the profession of the same Christian faith and conjoined in the communion of the same sacraments, under the government of the legitimate pastors, and especially the one vicar of Christ on earth, the Roman pontiff'. For Bellarmine the church is 'as visible and palpable as the community of the Roman people, or the Kingdom of France, or the Republic of Venice'. Under this view the boundaries of the church are defined by the reach of its rules, and welfare organisations are 'church' to the extent that they are under the control of the church hierarchy.

b) The church as mystical communion:
This model emphasises the relational dimension of the church, and welfare organisations are part of the church to the extent that they share the relational bonds of the church. Under this model whether the welfare agencies are part of the church depends a great deal on the type of people they employ—if they do not employ church members then the relational bonds which make the agency part of the church will wither.

c) The church as sacrament:
The symbolic function of the church is emphasised in this model, which has been promoted in the twentieth century by Henri de Lubac and Karl Rahner. All the churches' actions have symbolic value, but it is most concentrated in the eucharist. Under this model the welfare agencies are marginal to the church .

d) The church as herald:
The church's mission under this model is to proclaim the gospel, and welfare organisations are 'church' to the extent that they do this. In the twentieth century Karl Barth, and in his particular way Rudolf Bultmann, are representative, and it tends to be most popular among evangelical Protestants. Under this model welfare organisations that do not proclaim the gospel as they carry out their work are not church.

e) The church as servant:
The church here exists for those outside it, as emphasised by Dietrich Bonhoeffer and many others in the twentieth century. This model places the welfare agencies, with their serving mission, at the centre of the church.

The answer to the question of the relationship of the welfare agencies to the church and its mission depends on which of the above models is emphasised. The Roman Catholic Church tends to emphasise the first three models, evangelical Protestants the fourth and liberals of all traditions the fifth. On this basis we would expect to see a divergence of positions on contracting-out which flow from the divergent ecclesiologies of the parent churches with which the welfare organisations are associated. It is debatable whether we see this at the moment, and if it is not there, it would suggest that theology is not driving the responses of the welfare organisations to contracting-out. This suggestion is also supported by the dearth of theological reflection on contracting-out.

If theology is not driving the agencies' responses to contracting-out then what is? One possibility is that contracting-out offers the churches and their agencies a place in Australian society that they have not had for most of our history. Another is that contracting-out enhances the status and incomes of certain groups in the churches and agencies, and that this explains the enthusiasm for government contracts. Even if there are no gains for particular types of people driving the acceptance of government contracts there is no denying that the income from government contracts has been welcome as most mainline churches struggle financially.

5. Conclusions

Contracting-out of welfare and labour market services looks like being with us for the immediate future, irrespective of the result of the forthcoming election. The only thing that may change with a change of government is the position of religious welfare agencies in relation to secular agencies. If contracting is to be with us there are three main conclusions from this study.

First, there are important weaknesses from the point of view of regulatory economics with the current contracting arrangements. These weaknesses undermine economic efficiency and many of them will become worse over time. The most urgent issue is to modify the current arrangements to reduce the incentives to erode quality of service, for instance by moving away from fixed-price to cost-plus contracts. The arrangements should also be modified to ensure that the capacities of the agencies the government currently finds so attractive are not eroded. An important part of this would be to pay the agencies more for the services they provide. The effects of career incentives induced by contracting are important but more work on their precise effects is needed. The government also needs to be far more conscious of imperfect incentives for regulators and how this can lead to problems in the contracting process. I hope that some of the arguments in the economic concerns section of this paper will be useful to the agencies and others in arguing for improvements to the contracting process.

Second, the agencies need to think carefully about whether they should continue to bid for government contracts, especially if the necessary changes are not made to the process. Reasons for pulling out could be a pragmatic assessment that the contracts are not sufficiently profitable when all costs and risks are considered, or that taking the contracts is theologically problematic. Even if the theological concerns do not justify pulling out, I hope that the agencies will put their theological concerns forcefully to the government, and that these concerns will be addressed in the contracting process. There needs to be more of an equal partnership between the government and the agencies in the design of the arrangements. After all, if the government has moved to contracting in recognition of the superiority of the services provided by church welfare organisation it makes sense to listen to their views on how welfare should operate.

Third, if the agencies are to continue taking government contracts they need to think carefully about the way their organisations are structured. This includes both their relationship to the churches they are associated with, and the structure of incentives within the organisation. Structures which worked well when the welfare organisations were fairly autonomous will not necessarily work well in a contracting environment. Understanding and dealing with professionalisation and career structures should be a priority.

Besides these specific issues I believe the debate over contracting-out would be helped by the participants examining their own position more thoroughly. Those in the church welfare sector who reject market solutions on principle could think about the reasons for this. Economists need to be more aware of the limitations of their analytical tools, in particular their individualism and consequentialism, and be less hasty in condemning as nonsense arguments which are outside the reach of their analytical tools. Those in government need to be more aware of the subtleties of regulatory economics and the incentive problems which distort government action.

Finally, the process of undertaking an economic and theological evaluation has highlighted for me the weakness of our institutions in dealing with these issues. Contemporary mainstream economics excludes ethical and theological discourse, and when it encounters it, it tends to be hostile. The problem though is not just the culture of economics. In Australia there has been a sharp division in our education system between the secular universities (some of which are prohibited by their foundation documents to teach theology) and the theological colleges run by various churches which have traditionally focused on training their clergy. This division cuts down the possibilities for dialogue between theology and economics and impoverishes our public culture. Part of the confusion and anxiety over contracting-out seems to me to go back to these weaknesses in the cultures of contemporary economics and Australian public life.

6. Guide to Further Reading

6.1 Background
General material on the welfare state may be found in Barry
(1999) and Goodin (1998;2001), and the economics of the
welfare state is dealt with by Atkinson (1995;1999), Barr (1998),
and Saunders (1994). Thompson (1994) discusses the
involvement of the Australian churches, and Lyons (2001),
Industry Commission (1995) and Brown, Kenny, Turner and
Prince some current data on the welfare sector. The legal
context in which the churches operate is described by
McFarlane and Fisher (1996) and some legal issues with the
current arrangements are raised by Voyce (2001).

In the US, Olasky (1992), Sirocco (1993) and Mead (1997) are
representative of the calls for reform of welfare and Ellwood
(2001) provides a recent evaluation. Statements of the current
Australian government's position are Newman (1999) and
Abbott (2000), while McClure (2000) is the report commissioned
by the current government on welfare reform, with commentary by Dawkins (2001). Two important reports by the
quasi government body the Productivity Commission (previously named the Industry Commission) are Industry
Commission (1995;1996). Commentary by those associated with
the Australian welfare sector on the recent developments
includes de Carvalho (1994,1998), Honner (1998), Nevile (1999),
Ormerod (2000), Gregg (2000), Howe and O'Donnell (2000),
Sullivan and Davies (2000), and Considine (1996;2001). I have
found the work of Ann Nevile particularly thorough and
helpful on the impact on welfare agencies, and Neil Ormerod
and Samuel Gregg useful in highlighting some of the tensions
experienced by church agencies. Specifically on the Job Network there are a large number of documents produced by the
Department of Employment Workplace Relations and Small
Business and the evaluations of Kelly, Lewis, Mulvey, Norris
and Dockery (1999), Webster and Harding (2001) and the
Organisation for Economic Cooperation and Development
(2001). Independent evaluation of the Job Network has been un-
fortunately been hampered by confidentiality provisions of the
contracts and the extremely limited amount of data which has

been made publicly available. An inquiry by the Productivity Commission into the Job Network has just been announced.

6.2 *Why contracting-out?*
General discussions of contracting out in Australia are King (1994), Domberger (1994, 1998) and Industry Commission (1996) with critical commentary by Quiggin (1996).

The comments on economics of not-for profit enterprises are based on Rose-Ackerman (1986;1996), James and Rose-Ackerman (1986), and Weisbrod (1998). Some interesting points about the changed environment for not-for-profits in America are made by Ryan (1999).

6.3 *Economic concerns*
The philosophy and methodology of economics is a large and complex topic but a couple of readable introductions are Hausman (1989;1996). Perhaps the best way to understand the nature of economics is to read its history—for instance Heilbroner (1986) or Gordon (1991).

Textbook introductions to economic theory are Gans, King and Mankiw (1999), Milgrom and Roberts (1992) Varian (1993). Sen (1987) deals with the complexities of what it means to maximise welfare. On regulatory economics Laffont and Tirole (1993) is the standard reference work and Dixit (1997; 2000) provides readable recent overviews.

Incentives to erode quality are analysed in Laffont and Tirole (1993 ch4) and from the slightly different perspective of incomplete contracting by Hart (1996;1997). The problems of multiple agency are discussed by Dixit (1996 p98-104 and 1997). Maintaining long term competition is considered by Laffont and Tirole (1993 ch9-10). The recent literature on career concerns, especially in the public sector includes Holmstrom (1999), Dewatripont, Jewitt and Tirole (1999a; 1999b). The economics of advocacy is dealt with by Dewatripont and Tirole (1999), Tirole (1994) and Morris (2001). Discussions of monopsony power can be found in most textbooks of economic theory, for instance Varian (1993 p449-452). Some consequences of imperfect regulators are dealt with by Laffont and Tirole (1993 ch11,16) and Hart (1996;1997). This work on imperfect regulators draws on the larger literature on the economics of politics (known as public choice theory), for instance Stigler (1971), Tullock (1987), and Mueller (1989,1997).

6.4 Theological concerns

Good general material on the relationship between economics and theology includes the survey of Waterman (1987) and edited volume Brennan and Waterman (1994). Hay (1989) is a sensible attempt by an economist to bring the scriptures to bear on a wide range of economic issues, while Richardson (1988) emphasises the need for sound economic analysis by Christians. A fuller annotated list of references is in the student reading guide Oslington (1999), and my own views are sketched in a short conference paper (Oslington 2000).

The theological evaluation of markets has been a preoc-cupation of Catholic Social Teaching, surveyed by Charles (1998) and a sense of the debate in the Protestant churches can be gained from Gay (1991) and Hay (1989 ch4). In the churches the long tradition of hostility to markets exemplified by Tawney (1921;1937) and Milbank (1990), and the recent move in the other direction exemplified by Novak (1982;1993) and Griffiths (1982). Theological evaluations of the welfare state are Newbigin (1985), Biggar and Hay (1994), Mason (1987), Mason and Shaefer (1990), and chapters in the edited volume Carlson-Thies and Skillen (1996). Some works I have found helpful on the nature and mission of the church are Newbigin (1953), Dulles (1974), Stott (1983), Giles (1995) and Newbigin (1991). Economists work on the church is surveyed by Iannaccone (1998).

References

Abbott, T, Renewing the Social Fabric, *Policy* (Spring, 2000): 38-42.

Atkinson, A B, *Incomes and the Welfare State and Economic Performance* (Cambridge: Cambridge University Press, 1995).

Atkinson, A B, *The Economic Consequences of Rolling Back the Welfare State* (Cambridge, Massachusetts: Massachusetts Institute of Technology Press, 1999).

Barr, N A, *The Economics of the Welfare State* (Oxford: Oxford University Press, 1989).

Barry, N, *Welfare* (Buckingham: Open University Press, 1999).

Beed, C and C Beed, 'A Christian Perspective on Economics,' *Journal of Economic Methodology* 3 (1) 1996: 91-112.

Biggar, N and D Hay, 'The Bible Christian Ethics and the Provision of Social Security,' *Studies in Christian Ethics* 7 (2) 1994: 43-95.

Borland, J, 'Contracting Out: Some Labour Market Considerations,' *Australian Economic Review* (3) 1994: 86-90.

Brown, K M, S Kenny, B S Turner and J K Prince *Rhetorics of Welfare: Uncertainty, Choice and Voluntary Associations* (London: Macmillan, 2000).

Carlson-Thies, S W and J Skillen, *Welfare in America: Christian Perspectives on a Policy Crisis* (Grand Rapids: Eerdmans, 1996).

Charles, R, *Christian Social Witness and Teaching: The Catholic Tradition* (New York: Sheed and Ward, 1998).

Considine, M, 'Market Bureaucracy? Exploring the Contending Rationalities of Contemporary Administrative Regimes,' *Labour and Industry* 7 (1) 1996: 1-27.

Considine, M, *Enterprising States: The Public Management of Welfare to Work* (Melbourne: Cambridge University Press, 2001).

Dawkins, P, 'The Case for Welfare Reform as proposed by the McClure Report' *Australian Economic Review* 34 (1) 2001: 86-99.

de Carvalho, D, 'Does Charity Begin in the Market Place?' *Quadrant* (December) 1994: 29-33.

de Carvalho, D, *Competitive Care: Understanding the Implications of National Competition Policy and the COAG Agenda for the Community Services Sector* (Canberra: Australian Catholic Social Welfare Commission, 1998).

Department-of-Employment-Workplace-Relations-and-Small-Business, *Employment Services Tender Request and Draft Contract* (Canberra: AGPS, 1999).

Department-of-Employment-Workplace-Relations-and-Small-Business, *Job Network Evaluation Stage One: Implementation and Market Development* (Canberra: AGPS, 2000).

Department-of-Employment-Workplace-Relations-and-Small-Business, *The Future Purchasing of Job Network Services: Discussion Paper for Consultation* (Canberra: AGPS, 2001a).

Department-of-Employment-Workplace-Relations-and-Small-Business, *Job Network Evaluation Stage Two: Progress Report* (Canberra: AGPS, 2001b).

Dewatripont, M, I Jewitt and J Tirole, 'The Economics of Career Concerns, Part I: Comparing Information Structures,' *Review of Economic Studies* 66 (1) 1999a: 183-98.

Dewatripont, M, I Jewitt and J Tirole, 'The Economics of Career Concerns, Part II: Application to Missions and Accountability of Government Agencies,' *Review of Economic Studies* 66 (1) 1999b: 199-217.

Dewatripont, M and J Tirole, 'Advocates,' *Journal of Political Economy* 107 (1) 1999: 1-39.

Dixit, A K, *The Making of Economic Policy : A Transaction-Cost Politics Perspective* (Cambridge, Massachusetts: Massachusetts Institute of Technology Press, 1996).

Dixit, A K, 'Power of Incentives in Private vs Public Organizations,' *American Economic Review* 87 (2) 1997: 378-382.

Dixit, A K, *Incentives and Organizations in the Public Sector: An Interpretative Review*. Manuscript, 2000.

Domberger, S, 'Public Sector Contracting; Does it Work?' *Australian Economic Review* (3) 1994: 91-96.

Domberger, S, *The Contracting Organisation: A Strategic Guide to Outsourcing* (Oxford: Oxford University Press, 1998).

Dulles, A, *Models of the Church* (Dublin: Gill and Macmillan, 1974).

Ellwood, D T, 'The US Vision of Work Based Reform: Promise, Prospects and Pitfalls,' *Paper Presented at the National Social Policy Conference, UNSW* (July, 2001).

Gans, J, S King, S and M G N, *Principles of Economics*. (Melbourne: Harcourt Brace, 1999).

Gay, C M, *With Liberty and Justice for Whom? The Recent Evangelical Debate over Capitalism* (Grand Rapids: Eerdmans, 1991).

Giles, K, *What on Earth is the Church?* (Melbourne: Harper Collins, 1995).

Goodin, R, *Reasons for Welfare* (Princeton: Princeton University Press, 1988).

Goodin, R, *Whither the Welfare State*. Manuscript, 2001.

Gordon, S, *History and Philosophy of the Social Sciences* (London: Routledge, 1990).

Gregg, S, *Playing with Fire: Churches, Welfare Services and Government Contracts* (Sydney: Centre for Independent Studies, 2000), 1-8.

Griffiths, B, *Morality and the Market Place* (London: Hodder and Stoughton, 1982).

Hart, O, *Firms, Contracts and Financial Structure* (Oxford: Oxford University Press, 1995).

Hart, O, 'Privatisation and the Proper Scope of Government,' in *Industry Economics Conference Proceedings* (Canberra: Industry Commission, AGPS, 1996).

Hausman, D and M McPherson, *Economic Analysis and Moral Philosophy* (Cambridge: Cambridge University Press, 1996).

Hausman, D M, 'Economic Methodology in a Nutshell,' *Journal of Economic Perspectives* 3/1989: 115-27.

Hay, D A, *Economics Today: A Christian Critique* (Leicester: Apollos, 1989).

Hay, D A and D J Morris, *Industrial Economics: Theory and Evidence* (Oxford: Oxford University Press, 1990).

Heilbroner, R L, *The Worldly Philosophers: The Lives, Times, and Ideas of the Great Economic Thinkers* (New York: Simon & Schuster, 1986).

Holmstrom, B, 'Managerial Incentive Problems: A Dynamic Perspective,' *Review of Economic Studies* 66/1999: 169-182.

Honner, J, 'Contesting Welfare,' *Eureka Street* 8 (10) 1998: 29-33.

Howe, B and A O'Donnell, 'All Work and No Play?,' *Eureka Street* 10 (1) 2000: 87-90.

Iannaccone, L, 'Introduction to the Economics of Religion,' *Journal of Economic Literature* 36 (3) 1998: 1465-1495.

Industry Commission, *Charitable Organisations in Australia* (Canberra: AGPS, 1995) Available from their web site http://www.pc,gov.au.

Industry Commission, *Competitive Tendering and Contracting by Public Sector Agencies* (Canberra: AGPS, 1996). Available from their web site http://www.pc,gov.au.

James, E and S Rose-Ackerman, *The NonProfit Enterprise in Market Economies* (Chur: Harwood Academic Publishers, 1986).

Kelly, R P Lewis, C Mulvey, K Norris and M Dockery, *The Job Network: Is it Working?* (Canberra: Committee for the Economic Development of Australia, 1999).

King, S, 'Competitive Tendering and Contracting Out: An Introduction,' *Australian Economic Review* (3) 1994: 75-77.

Laffont, J J and J Tirole, *A Theory of Incentives in Procurement and Regulation* (Cambridge and London: Massachusetts Institute of Technology Press, 1993).

Lyons, M, *Third Sector: The Contribution of NonProfit and Cooperative Enterprises in Australia* (Sydney: Allen and Unwin, 2001).

Mason, J D, 'Biblical Teaching on Assisting the Poor,' *Transformation* 4 (April) 1987 1-14.

Mason, J D and K C Schaefer 'The Bible, the State and the Economy: A Framework for Analysis,' *Christian Scholars Review* 20 (1) 1990: 45-64.

McClure, P, *Participation Support for a More Equitable Society: Final Report of the Reference Group on Welfare Reform* (Canberra: AGPS, 2000).

McFarlane, P and S Fisher, *Churches, Clergy and the Law* (Sydney: Federation Press, 1996).

Mead, L, *The New Paternalism: Supervisory Approaches to Poverty* (Washington: Brookings Institute, 1997).

Milbank, J, *Theology and Social Theory: Beyond Secular Reason* (Oxford: Basil Blackwell, 1990).

Milgrom, P and J Roberts, *Economics, Organization and Management* (New York: Prentice Hall, 1992).

Morris, S (2001) 'Political Correctness,' *Journal of Political Economy* 109(2): 231-265.

Mueller, D C, *Public Choice II* (Cambridge: Cambridge University Press, 1989).

Mueller, D C, ed, *Perspectives on Public Choice* (Cambridge: Cambridge University Press, 1997).

Nevile, A, *Competing Interests: Competition in the Welfare Sector* (Canberra: The Australia Institute and Anglicare Australia, 1999).

Newbigin, L, *The Household of God* (London: SCM Press, 1953).

Newbigin, L, 'The Welfare State: A Christian Perspective,' *Theology* 88/1985: (723).

Newbigin, L, *Truth to Tell: The Gospel as Public Truth* (Grand Rapids: Eerdmans, 1991).

Newman, J, *The Future of Welfare in the 21st Century*, Speech to the National Press Club, Canberra 29 September, 1999.

Novak, M, *The Spirit of Democratic Capitalism* (New York: Simon and Schuster, 1982).

Novak, M, *In Praise of the Free Economy: Essays by Michael Novak* (Sydney: Centre for Independent Studies, 1999).

Olasky, M, *The Tragedy of American Compassion* (Chicago: Regnery, 1992).

Organisation for Economic Cooperation and Development, *Innovations in Labour Market Policies-The Australian Way* (Paris: OECD, 2001), Available at www.oecd.org/media/publish.

Ormerod, N, 'Drawing the Line,' *Eureka Street* 10 (2) 2000: 14-15.

Oslington, P, *Theology and Economics: A Reading Guide.* (Melbourne: Zadok Institute, 1999). The Zadok Institute web site is: http://www.zadok.org.au/.

Oslington, P, 'A Theological Economics,' *International Journal of Social Economics* 27 (1) 2000: 32-44. Reprinted in *Journal of the UK Association of Christian Economists* 27 (March) 2000:17-31, and available on their web site: http://users.aber.ac.uk/arh/ace.html.

Oslington, P, ed, (forthcoming) *Economics and Religion.* International Library of Critical Writings in Economics (Cheltenham: Edward Elgar).

Oslington, P (forthcoming) in 'God and Economic Order: Natural Theology in the Political Economy of Smith, Malthus and their Followers'.

Paul Oslington

Quiggin, J, *Great Expectations: Microeconomic Reform and Australia* (Sydney: Allen and Unwin, 1996).

Richardson, J D, 'Frontiers in Economics and Christian Scholarship,' *Christian Scholars Review* 17 (4) 1988: 381-400. Reprinted in *Journal of the UK Association of Christian Economists* (March) 1988:1-20 and *US Association of Christian Economists Bulletin* 23 (Spring) 1994: 16-36. Their web site is: http://www. gordon.edu/ace/

Rose-Ackerman, S, *The Economics of Nonprofit Institutions: Studies in Structure and Policy* (New York: Oxford University Press, 1986).

Rose-Ackerman, S, 'Altruism, NonProfits and Economic Theory,' *Journal of Economic Literature* 43 (2) 1996: 701-728.

Ryan, W P, 'The New Landscape for NonProfits,' *Harvard Business Review* (January) 1999: 127-136.

Saunders, P, *Welfare and Inequality* (Cambridge: Cambridge University Press, 1994).

Sen, A, 'Social Choice,' in *The New Palgrave: A Dictionary of Economics* edited by J Eatwell, M Milgate and P Newman (London: Macmillan, 1987).

Siroco, R, *Economics, Faith and Moral Responsibility* (Sydney: Centre for Independent Studies, 1993).

Stigler, G, 'The Theory of Economic Regulation,' *Bell Journal of Economics and Management Science* 2 (1) 1971: 1-21.

Stott, J R W, *Issues Facing Christians Today* (London: Marshalls, 1983).

Sullivan, F and L Davies, eds, *Civilising Community for Us All* (Adelaide: Australian Theological Forum, 2000).

Tawney, R H, *The Acquisitive Society* (London: Bell, 1921).

Tawney, R H, *Religion and the Rise of Capitalism* (Harmondsworth: Penguin, 1937).

Thompson, R C (1994) *Religion in Australia: A History* (Melbourne: Oxford University Press, 1994).

Tirole, J, 'The Internal Organization of Government,' *Oxford Economic Papers* 46/1994:1-29.

Tullock, G , 'Public Choice' in *The New Palgrave: A Dictionary of Economics* edited by J Eatwell, M Milgate and P Newman (London: Macmillan, 1987).

Varian, H, *Microeconomic Analysis* (New York: Norton, 1993).

Voyce, M, *Unemployment Benefits and the Transition from Work to Welfare in a Market Economy: The Role of Tony Abbott and the Churches* (Sydney: Division of Law, Macquarie University, 2001).

Waterman, A M C, 'Economists on the Relation between Political Economy and Christian Theology: A Preliminary Survey,' *International Journal of Social Economics* 14 (6) 1987: 46-68.

Webster, E and G Harding, 'Outsourcing Public Employment Services: The Australian Experience,' *Australian Economic Review* (June) 2001: 231-242.

Weisbrod, B, ed, *To Profit or Not to Profit: The Commercial Transformation of the NonProfit Sector* (New York: Cambridge University Press, 1998).

Questions for Group Discussion for Welfare Agency Staff

1. In your opinion, why does the government find contracting–out and which of the means given do you think is most important?

2. From your experience working in a welfare organisation, what assessment was done in the possible impact of accepting government contracts—positive and negative? What would a full assessment of costs and benefits look like?

3. What impact has contracting out had on recipients of welfare and labour market services?

4. How do you define 'quality' in the sector in which you work? To what extent is it observable by the recipient, the welfare organisation and a third party? To what extent is quality verifiable?

5. Describe the career structures and incentives in the welfare sector. Is reputation important for career progression and how is it established? What has been the impact of contracting-out on these processes?

6. Do you think welfare organisations should be involved with advocacy? Who would benefit? How?

7. What are your views on 'markets' and the 'state'. Are these views shared by most of the people you work with? How were they formed? Do the views affect the way that you work within the organisation and with those with whom you work?

8. Do you consider welfare organisations to be part of the church? How does this affect an assessment of contracting out?

Justice at the Core of Mission

Ray Cleary

> You who fatten yourselves and enjoy your ease.
> You who drink well into the night, and then
> cover yourselves with soft blankets . . . you dare
> demand a strict account for the needy who is
> little more than a corpse, and you fear not the
> account you will have to render before the court
> of Christ, terrible and frightful. If the poor fake,
> it is out of need that they fake, for it is your
> merciless inhumanity and your cruelty that
> forces them to do so.[1]

Many Christians express concern, some even outrage when church and community leaders challenge and debate with political and corporate leaders economic and social policy which victimises or marginalises sections of the community. In a similar vein when leaders of faith-based welfare agencies do likewise they are often reminded by government not to become 'political' and to remember their contractual obligations.

Christians often express a one sided or singular view about salvation, stating that the saving work of God is only personal in intent and has no significant communal agenda. It is not that Christians are unaware that God's love and justice is for all of creation and that the generosity of spirit is unconditional, but they rather limit this hospitality by dogma which binds up rather than liberates the human person.

The story of God's encounters with the human family as told in Scripture tell of a deep compassion for justice in the Creator's agenda for communal life—a life enriched by the values of compassion, mercy, forgiveness and reconciliation. The ministry,

---

1. John Chrysostom, 4th Century Archbishop of Constantinople.

death and resurrection of Jesus is the fulfilment of this promise. The cross of Christ is the sign of God's justice and compassion, freely given for the purpose of reconciliation with God and between members of the human family.

The principle of this encounter and event is exemplified in the parable of the Good Samaritan and is incarnated in the words 'you shall love your neighbour as yourself'. Acceptance of this claim provides a rationale and focus for pursuing a threefold mission agenda, namely proclamation, adoration and service, each together affirming the presence of God in the world. It allows the church and its welfare agencies to embrace both Matthew's call to share the Good News to everyone and Isaiah's hope as told in Luke 4:16 as the vision for the church to build a just and compassionate community. Affirmed then in the resurrection of Jesus is the ongoing struggle for justice, an agenda which is both personal and social. Our participation in God's justice means we share in the meaning of resurrection today.

Jesus embodies inspiration and hope for Christians. He is the celebrated light of the world and provides the means by which Christians understand their relationship with God. In Jesus, God's agenda is set before us. His story provides the framework for the mission of the church and its welfare obligation. It does not follow on from belief, it is the essence of belief, 'to love God and to love one's neighbour'.

The beginning for many church agencies was linked with the evangelical/conversion motive to save souls. Poverty, drunkenness and idleness were seen as a result of individual moral decadence and irresponsibility.

They were considered the outcomes of poor personal choices. Help or support was often only given after the individuals had confessed their sins, acknowledged their depravity and sought forgiveness from Jesus. Help or support was also disbursed according to moral judgments of deserving and undeserving. In practice children were deserving and women were not. A number of these practices persisted until the late 1960's, and remnants of these values are often not far from the surface in some agencies even today.

Typical of church involvement in the depression of the late 1920s was the movement to save slum babies that led to the erection of the Methodist Babies' Home in 1929.

> Some of the young men have been challenged by the slum conditions that exist at our very doors, and it has been decided, after very careful consideration, to take up the challenge and attempt some very definite work to counteract the dreadful menace of slum life. [2]

It is dangerous and too simplistic to evaluate past practices described above as judgmental and inappropriate. The actions of the early missionaries and workers were consistent with the beliefs and common practice of that time. This is not to excuse, but to understand. It is to recognise that today we stand with greater knowledge and the experience of hindsight. By today's understanding, it is clear that discrimination occurred. Babies born out of wedlock were to be taken from their mothers and placed in new families for their own good and protection. The natural mother's own needs and identity were secondary and less deserving.[3] The natural father was rarely identified or part of the discussion.

Dr Len Tierney in a Paper he presented in 1962, suggests that:

> Part of a stimulus to preach the gospel came about as a reaction to a great deal of

---

2.   P Tinney, Copelen Street, Evaluation Report, Melbourne 1999, (iii).

3.   The Stolen Generation debate in Australia at the present time clearly articulates the pain and suffering which occurred to Aboriginal Australians when their children were taken from them by highly motivated and sincere white Australians. Many who supported such policies were Christian. These actions are now the subject of passionate debate within the community.

intemperance and degraded behaviour which
went hand in hand with great poverty, poor
medical care and illiteracy. [4]

The early 1970's saw the term 'community welfare' introduced,
which by the 1980's became 'Community Services', as the word
welfare at the time was seen as having derogatory and discri-
minatory overtones. With the introduction of super ministries
at both Federal and State Government levels in the 1990's, the
terms 'Community Services' and 'Community Welfare' were
gradually replaced with the names 'Family and Community' or
'Human Services'.

1. Current Status

The church in Australia and, in particular, church welfare
agencies have played a significant role in the development of
welfare services in Victoria since the 1840's. Presently, church
welfare agencies share with government, and other community
organisations, the goal of building a just and compassionate
society. Essential to this relationship has been a commitment to
a shared partnership and an agreed vision, although the latter
more by implication than by written statement. This shared
partnership has involved a recognition by government of the
role the church historically has played in providing welfare
programs. Services provided have included residential homes
for babies and children, adoption and foster care programs,
hostels and nursing homes for older citizens and people with
disabilities, drug treatment programs, employment and
training opportunities and refuges for women and the
homeless.

The new competitive environment introduced in the early
1990's has challenged and threatened existing partnerships and
created a different context for church welfare agencies and their
role in serving those in need. The effects of these threats and
challenges are now examined in greater detail and suggest that

---

4.   L J Tierney, *The Church and Social Welfare—the historical background*,
      unpublished paper delivered to the Victorian Council of Churches consultation on
      Social Welfare, 1962, 3.

the future role of church welfare agencies may be vastly different from their past and present contribution.

2. New Concerns
The threats and challenges have been emerging for some time. It would be too simplistic to see them as grounded only in the impact of globalisation and the radical resurgence of market economics. They are also a result of the increasing professionalisation of the community sector, greater media interest, changing government agenda and welfare weariness expressed in some quarters. In this changing environment the challenge for church welfare agencies is to remain faithful to their Christ-given mission, while responding to emerging community needs and changing expectations.

Paul Oslington in Chapter 1 discusses why churches and their agencies are attractive to government as service deliverers. He identifies a number of reasons, and also why some church agencies participate with government in pursuing a new welfare agenda, embracing competitive tendering and the principles of deserving and undeserving, welfare targeting, mutual obligation and co-option of the church welfare agency into the government's agenda.

Oslington also rightly points out many church agencies are unhappy about this trend and have taken stands opposed to this creeping seduction or co-option depending upon their place along the theological spectrum. Others, he notes, participate with intent. Oslington deals only marginally with the essence of theological debate on how and why the churches should engage with society, concentrating on economic issues, ignoring the place of justice as an essential part of the church welfare agency mission. Instead he advances a number of important economic considerations that need attention in defining a church agency and government partnership. This he states as the primary purpose of his paper. His discussion, however, does not link the church's agenda for the building of a just community with the paradigm of market economics on the possibility of meeting common goals.

The shift from charity to the justice model of many of present church welfare agencies began in the early 1970's. New welfare practices and research contributed to a shift in the way agencies responded to the causes of unemployment and poverty. The shift in practice recognised the significant role played by the social environment, and lack of employment opportunities, education, housing and health support in creating conditions which impact on the lives of individuals. In the current climate, reduced funding for public hospitals and increasing demands for health services as the population ages create longer public hospital waiting lists, and impacts particularly on low income people and those unable to afford private health insurance.

Likewise, the withdrawal of welfare officers in schools reduces the chances that presenting difficulties, such as homelessness amongst young people, can be prevented. Reduction in funds for dental services means that families on low incomes and those on social security benefits are likely to miss out on much needed treatment.

3. Welfare and the Market

Many church welfare and community agencies have increasingly recognised how government policies, and the strategies of corporate organisations, within a market ideology, can impact on the lives of a community. Agencies acknowledge and affirm that the unemployed do not create unemployment. The lack of job opportunities is a direct result of government and business policies which are designed to improve Australia's economic performance and to place the nation strategically in the global market.

These strategies, however, do have their fall-out and have created major shifts in employment, housing, health and social security needs. As a result, agencies have responded with service provision, and have taken increasingly strong advocacy positions on behalf of those affected by the change. The commitment to advocacy has raised new issues for many church welfare agencies and brought to the surface questions about economic and social goals. Further, it has raised important questions of the relationship between government as funder and agency as provider. In some cases it goes to challenging the heart of the agency's mission.

As increasing numbers of people lose out in the new economic world, many church welfare agencies and their leaders are becoming more vocal, challenging both governments and the community to a higher level of responsibility and expenditure. The response of many church welfare agencies is to challenge prevailing economic goals and models which promote the creation of wealth as an end in itself, and which understand the market as the predominant or sole determiner and arbiter of demand and supply. Many of the agencies advocate government intervention in markets which discriminate against individuals and argue for a just sharing and distribution of the common wealth.

4. Service and Justice
Social justice should not be confused with charity or good works. It is not that both charity and good works are wrong but they are only part of the answer. Charity relieves symptoms. Social justice addresses and seeks solutions to issues of poverty, homelessness, abuse and lack of housing. Social justice involves both the giving of resources and one's self for the kingdom of God. Social justice is not about welfare programs; it is about the building of community, respect for human dignity and self-worth, a fair share and distribution of resources, and the search for wholeness. Welfare programs are a means of achieving this goal. The practice of social justice for church welfare agencies is about the naming of God, the recognition of the divine in the 'least of my brothers and sisters' and applies equally within the Church as in the wider community. Social justice involves listening to the pain, distress and humiliation associated with poverty, unemployment, homelessness, abuse and drug dependence. It is about the embodiment of God's kingdom.

Responding to these issues means engaging in the politics of life, challenging sacred political ideologies and sharing what we ourselves possess. At times this may mean experiencing the hurt and pain of those who are marginalised. It means not embracing policies or programs which seek to blame, victimise or control the destiny of those on the margins of society.

Instead, the task is to express in word and deed the overflowing and generous nature of God's love, not by concentrating on blame, weakness or poor choices, but rather seeking to build on strengths and possibilities. It involves a commitment to the sharing of resources of both the community and nation.

4.1 Revelation and justice

In the Christian tradition, justice comes from the Hebrew, s'daqah meaning God's fidelity to right relationships built upon the idea of covenant. This notion of covenant begins in the Hebrew Scriptures with Abraham. The idea of covenant binds God to the act of unconditional love and calls humankind to be faithful to God's providence. The Exodus story is evidence of covenant, despite the fact that the people of Israel in their frustration and disappointment seek to break it down.

Throughout the New Testament, the covenant imagery continues, culminating in the death and resurrection of Jesus as the healer of the brokenness and separation of humanity from God. This healing occurs as a result of God's generosity and heartache for reconciliation. Jesus, the victim, offers forgiveness and reveals the fullness of God's love.

Essential to covenant are social relationships. Justice, involving the commitment to living in harmony and balance with all of creation is to be the out-working of God's own covenant with humankind 'To do justice, to love kindness and to walk humbly with your God' as proclaimed by the prophet Micah, becomes the working out of God's continuing self-disclosure.[5]

Where the commitment to God's justice is absent or marginalised by the actions of individuals, social and economic policies, the fulfilment of God's love is diminished by this

---

5.   Micah 6:8.

action. God, however, remains faithful to those offended, despite our failure.

5. St Luke—A Model of Social Justice

Luke's Gospel provides a model for a church welfare agency's engagement in issues which affect communities, a model consistent with God's call for a just kingdom. Luke's Gospel provides a revisioning approach. Luke is constantly interpreting the scriptures and the Jesus tradition within the experiences of his faith community. Luke has been chosen because his Gospel reflects the ethic of love grounded in service, not privilege. This ethic is centred on the importance of relationships in defining who we are, in particular, our relationship with God and with each other. Luke's Gospel has also been chosen because his narrative is one of both struggle and reflection.

Luke describes his own community of faith as grounded in orthodoxy, but changing and emerging with new understandings as the Jesus movement of the time gained prominence and strength. Luke's community had similarities to the experiences of many today. In the post-modern experience, the ease with which agencies can forget or misplace the significance of the Jesus story is real. The pressures on agencies to conform to emerging ideologies and restrictive agendas is a threat. To be constantly aware of these dangers is essential. But the challenges and threats are not just from the outside. They also come from within, both the agency and theology itself.

Luke's Gospel undertakes the task of relating the experiences of his community to the emerging Jesus tradition. Luke examines what the Christian faith community is called to be, one based on Christ Himself. Hope and promise in the resurrected and ascended Christ is open to all and discipleship calls us to live in the world, to renew community and the creation together.

6. An Overview of Luke's Gospel

Luke's Gospel is enriching, informative and constructive in detailing and articulating the benchmarks or criteria by which the church welfare agency may seek to respond to the social and ethical issues it confronts. Luke is concerned with Jesus' mission in establishing and proclaiming God's, community or kingdom. God's Kkngdom, according to Luke, is to be a place of harmony, a manifestation of the fullness of God's love built on compassion and inclusive relationships which reflect the very nature of God's being. For Luke the kingdom is greater than a moral or ritual behaviour guide. Luke's ethic of love springs from the very nature of God as one who, in the act of creation, willed the existence of the known universe. God's kingdom is to be a present reality and Jesus the sign of its manifestation. This ethic of love and justice is to be expressed in partnership with those who call themselves followers or disciples. Luke's Jesus calls his followers to proclaim the day of the Lord and the source of compassion as springing from God's justice.

The Gospel writer presents responses to social and ethical issues which enrich and develop relationships within the human family based on God's enduring and faithful justice. Luke's Gospel helps us identify acts of discrimination against the poor, women and the marginalised. The writer of Luke challenges attitudes and policies contrary to God's love and kingdom, and the Gospel provides a substantial answer to those who claim they can live a good life without any need of God.

Luke's response is to draw on the rich religious traditions of the past, presenting an ethic of love which, while common to other religious traditions, is grounded in the Hebrew faith and in the active ministry of Jesus. The 'Word made Flesh' becomes the model for a response to acts of discrimination and abuse in today's world. God's presence is a living reality and involves struggle and rejection in building a just community.

For the welfare agency which seeks to remain faithful to participating with God in this journey, the mission is open to risk and adversity. Understood in this way, the agency's role as service provider and advocate is to embody God's plan for an ongoing relationship with all. In the struggles the agencies face, new opportunities arise for different ways of responding to the social and ethical issues of today.

Central to the Lukan narrative are three themes: the poor, justice and the inclusive community—the kingdom of God. The essential elements of Luke's Gospel, which are important in understanding his approach to the ethical issues of the day, may be described in the following way:

- First Luke's narrative is clearly placed within the history of Israel and the community's journey and relationship with the God of Abraham, Isaac and Jacob. Luke understands Jesus as standing within this prophetic tradition and as the fulfilment of Israel's messianic claims.
- Second, Luke, throughout his account illustrates God's special concern for the poor and marginalised by affirming their exalted place, while the rich and powerful are reprimanded and berated.
- Third, Luke's 'rhetorical method' as it is described is continually emphasised throughout the Gospel, with each new story, parable or account adding a dimension to the life and ministry of Jesus, as a demonstration of God's justice and faithfulness.
- Fourth, Luke uses imagery from the Hebrew Scriptures and blends his themes of justice and mercy throughout his account of the Jesus story to demonstrate the nature of true and faithful discipleship.
- Fifth, Luke is well versed in the Septuagint[6] and the traditions surrounding Jesus. He integrates them both into the text to strengthen his own

---

6.   Septuagint is the Greek translation of the Old Testament, from about 150AD.

understanding and to highlight to those who
oppose him, their lack of scriptural commitment
to their own faith.[7]

Luke takes the literary images and the memory of the Jesus
movement and with the skill of the artist weaves them into a
powerful and dramatic account of God's faithfulness and
justice. In the view of Luke, Jesus is the fulfilment of this
promise.

Luke's presentation of the ministry of Jesus and the
description of his engagement with the communities of his time
provides a powerful model for the church welfare agency
today. Building on the Christian tradition as its starting point,
and affirming the place of Jesus as central to tradition, the
church welfare agency has, in Luke's account, a model of
engagement readily available which can honour the past, yet
integrate and weave a faith perspective and ethic of love into
the context of the times. This mode of engagement allows
revisioning and reflection on the scriptures, history and tradition of the Church in a constructive and relevant manner.

Luke's Jesus is presented as a very human person,
knowledgeable of the scriptures and with a deep passion and
concern for the poor and the marginalised. Likewise is the task
of the agency. In the Sermon on the Plain, the reader is
conscious of the failure of the religious and political leaders of
the day to address inequality, and the challenge to them to
repent of their ways and to enact the justice and faithfulness of
God. The tensions and conflicts of the community are
immediately identified and the solutions reinforced. The Beatitudes see the commencement of the Lukan theme of journey,
which has its beginning in the prologue (Luke 1:1-4), and is

---

7.   L Johnson, *The Gospel of Luke*, Sacra Pagina, edited by D J Harrington
      (Liturgical Press, Minnesota: Liturgical Press, 1991), 4. The author describes
      Luke's original contribution to Christian literature 'connecting the events of the
      early church to those of Jesus' ministry and to the whole Story of God's people,
      indeed of humanity, all the way back to Adam'.

articulated in both Mary's song (1:46-55) and the anointing by the Spirit in 4:16.

Luke draws on the richness of the Septuagint and tradition to outline the justice and faithfulness of God, identifying the poor and the marginalised as having a special place in God's Kingdom. The journey narrative which follows, particularly Chapters 9—19, plays out the teachings of repentance, responsibility and promise to the marginalised referred to in the beatitudes. The elements of covenant are articulated and reaffirmed. The sermon clearly articulates the following central themes of Luke's Jesus. They are:

- the lowly and mighty are contrasted
- the constant call for repentance
- the cost of discipleship which involves suffering and humiliation
- a statement of ethical standards essential for community life
- the authority of Jesus as agent of God.

These themes are then interwoven by Luke with the memory of Israel's prophetic past and journey, to present a living account of Jesus as the faithful prophet of God who is to suffer in order to be vindicated by God. As Danker says, 'God is creator of all, merciful to all and judge of all'.[8]

Luke's exposition of these themes is to present the essence of defining right relationships necessary for the restoration of God's covenant rather than a moral code fixed for all time. The emphasis is to be on right relationships and to be interpreted, as Luke demonstrates by his own style, contextually. The conclusions to be drawn from the discussion on Luke's Sermon on the Plain may be summarised as follows:

---

8.   F Danker, *Luke Proclamation Commentaries*, edited by G Krodel (Philadelphia: Fortress Press, 1987), 3.

Luke's Jesus is God's righteous and faithful prophet who appeals to the Lukan community as the fulfilment of Israel's messianic expectations. In Jesus the covenant relationship is restored and the Kingdom of God is proclaimed as a present opportunity and reality. Luke is not concerned with the 'spiritualised' poor as is Matthew, but rather the marginalised and destitute. At the same time the challenge is to those who have status and wealth to give all away, to redistribute resources and to follow in the footsteps of God's justice. For Luke, good news for the poor is to be seen in the life of Jesus, and the invitation to them to be present at God's banquet is confirmation of this pronouncement. Salvation, for Luke, is in the actions of justice and compassion, following in the footsteps of Jesus, as God's agent and servant. The kingdom has arrived.

7. Themes Emerging from Luke's Gospel

Building on the substance of Luke's Gospel, and in particular the Sermon on the Plain, themes central to the future role of church welfare agencies can be identified.

The themes to be discussed are justice and salvation, the poor, the prophetic tradition, the rich and powerful, commensality (table fellowship), the kingdom of God and jubilee.

7.1 Justice and salvation: a reversal of destinies

Luke proclaims the content of God's justice and salvation early in his Gospel account in the words of Mary's song:

> My soul magnifies the Lord, and my spirit rejoices in God my saviour, for he has regarded the low estate of his handmaiden. For behold, henceforth all generations will call me blessed; for he who is mighty has done great things for me, and holy is his name. And mercy is on those who fear him, from generation to generation. He has shown strength with his arm, he has scattered the proud in the imagination of their hearts, he has put down the mighty from their thrones, and exalted those of low degree; he has filled the hungry with good things, and the rich he has sent

empty away. He has helped his servant Israel, in remembrance of his mercy, as he spoke to our fathers, to Abraham and to his posterity forever.[9]

Here we see one of Luke's main literary devices designed to present his message clearly. The Magnificat outlines a reversal of destinies that Luke incorporates throughout his narrative. It points not to Jesus, but beyond to God, to an understanding of God's Kingdom as a sign of God's justice. The passage points not to wealth and status, but rather to servanthood and discipleship as key elements of God's kingdom. The Sermon on the Plain presents the same radical demands as found in the Magnificat.

7.2 The poor

Who then are the poor and the marginalised Luke speaks about? Unlike Matthew's account of the Sermon on the Plain, the poor are not spiritualised in Luke's Gospel. Luke builds his argument for the special place within God's plan for the poor by reference to Jubilee in the history of Israel. God's Jubilee claims freedom and victory for the poor, release for the captives, and sight for the blind. Luke links his understanding of being poor with the words of the prophet Isaiah and his poor are to be understood in both an economic and social context. The poor are poor because they are hungry, unemployed and marginalised. Their poverty and exclusion is not to be resolved in a future still to come, but is to be addressed in the present by the sharing of resources, and by inclusion in the life of the community. Food for the hungry, shelter for the homeless and comfort to the sojourner are to be the responsibility of all who follow in the footsteps of Jesus.

Concern for the poor is a predominant theme in Luke's narrative. First introduced in the Magnificat, elaborated further in the baptismal story in the temple in Luke 4, and reiterated in more detail in the Sermon on the Plain, this theme provides the basis for the expression of the community's responsibility. Each

---

9.   Luke 1:46-55, known as 'The Magnificat or Mary's song'.

of the parables in Luke chapters 9—19 elaborates and describes elements of God's justice and faithfulness.

These Chapters demonstrate that Luke's Jesus has a deep passion for the poor, to be understood as a direct consequence of God's beneficence and generosity. The good news to be preached to the poor is that their condition is to be improved. They are to be valued, while those who have accumulated wealth and power and not exercised compassion and responsibility are guilty of rejecting the justice of God. The consequence is their rejection by God. The message is a clear and direct call to repentance to those who have violated the law and tradition. It is also a call to the restoration of the covenant relationship between God and fellow travellers.

Luke seeks to recall the memory of Israel's faith as evidence for his claims, and as the framework for the teachings of Jesus. Luke intends that we should be talking about the real poor in economic and political terms in contrast to the real rich. Jesus constantly invites the poor to table fellowship while at the same time warning the rich and powerful that they, by their very actions, have excluded themselves from such fellowship.[10] In common fellowship around the table, God's justice is celebrated. All are welcome, and in particular those who are currently excluded and on the outside.

7.3 *The prophetic tradition*

Luke's concern for the poor and the marginalised shown in declaring God's kingdom a present reality places Jesus clearly within Israel's prophetic tradition. Luke builds on the place of prophetic tradition and experience in the Hebrew Scriptures in his telling of the Jesus story. Luke's Jesus is depicted as the prophet of God who, in continuity with the Hebrew prophets, seeks to restore the covenant relationship between individuals, com-munity and God.

Like the earlier prophets of the Hebrew Scriptures, Jesus demonstrates the call to righteousness and justice as central to

---

10.   See Luke 14: 15-24.

discipleship. One cannot fully understand Luke's Jesus, his mission, his place within Israel's faith and his relationship with God, without understanding this connection with the prophetic tradition. The call to repentance, and the place of salvation within the Lukan approach, can only be fully understood from this vantage point.

It is in the context of this prophetic tradition that Luke has Jesus marginalised and crucified because he identifies himself with the poor and broken.

The call by Luke's Jesus to repentance and the sharing of worldly goods was clearly an affront and challenge to the power-brokers of the time. Repentance and the sharing of one's wealth presented within the context of the faith of Israel was an explicit reminder to the religious leaders of the day of their obligation under the law. In the end, for many, these demands were too great. The religious leaders had Jesus crucified.

In grounding the ministry of Jesus within the prophetic tradition, Luke's Jesus confirms the faithfulness of God's justice and generosity. Jesus, God's righteous and just prophet, ultimately pays with his life for being faithful to God. Jesus is the spokesperson for God's righteousness. The call, then, to the community to which Luke is writing was to put their faith in this person Jesus. In Jesus, the themes of poverty, repentance and prophecy were contextually linked. The traditions and teachings of Judaism were critiqued, and the memory of Israel's past relived and proclaimed as the way to God and the establishment of the kingdom, here and now.

This prophetic overview as outlined in Luke provides a framework and context for Luke's Jesus to build on history, and scripture. Jesus, God's prophet of justice, lives out the prophetic tradition as one who is rejected and suffers.

7.4 Commensality[11]

To this theme of prophecy, Luke then adds commensality, to be understood as table fellowship. For Luke's Jesus, entrance to the banquet is open to all who seek to live according to God's principles of justice and righteousness. Participation in table fellowship is vindication of God's compassion. God offers the kingdom to those who are marginalised. The invitation to share the table (commensality) demonstrates the seriousness of God's compassion and justice for the marginalised. Luke's Jesus is the one who announces this vision of God. It is the central theme of the Sermon on the Plain. The introduction of the theme of commensality clearly brings into play the Lukan theme of inclusiveness.

7.5 The rich and powerful

But what does Luke then have to say about the rich and powerful? Throughout his narrative, and particularly in the Sermon on the Plain with Luke's inclusion of the 'woes' as part of his text, the rich and powerful are seen to have contributed significantly to the problems being experienced in the community. They have more resources than they need. They have created boundaries around access to the temple and God. Their laws and rituals have excluded those who are unable to fulfil their temple obligations because of their economic and social circumstances.

It is the powerful and rich who subvert justice and who by their actions create barriers to commensality, the sharing of table fellowship.

Who are the powerful and rich? Luke portrays the Pharisees as those who 'neglect justice and the love of God'.[12] They are powerful and they preside over the riches of the temple. They perform religious rituals and preside over temple practices.

---

11.   Commensality derives from commensalism, a relationship between two
       individuals of different species in which one lives on or off the other; similar to
       symbiosis. Commensality has come to be used theologically to mean table
       fellowship where one is dependent on the other.

12.   Luke 11:42b.

Luke's portrayal of the conflict between the religious authorities and Jesus, may also be understood as representing the conflicts within Luke's own community over issues of resources, shared responsibility, adherence to the law and membership of both the temple and the new emerging Jesus movement. Eating with sinners, healing on the Sabbath, engaging with outcasts became hot issues of the day. Wealth is linked with status and power and these are clearly identified as evil and a barrier to the justice of God. Luke's Jesus calls on those with authority and wealth to share their riches with those least well off.

7.6 The kingdom
The beatitudes in the Sermon on the Plain echo the refrain that the mighty will be brought low and the lowly raised. This is the centrepiece of Luke's reversal motif. It is a sign and a symbol of Luke's kingdom.[13] Trainor and others indicate this reversal motif as central to Luke's understanding of community, challenging wealth, status, exclusiveness and prejudice, all of which have the effect of excluding many from full participation in community life.[14]

The reign, or kingdom of God, challenges the aspects of community life which bring about poverty, hunger and alienation. Luke seeks to connect Israel's understanding of Jubilee with his Kingdom theology in addressing the plight of the poor and those on the outside. Jubilee, which involved the cancelling of debts, the restoration of people to their land and the establishment of right relationships, was to be an expression of Israel's social responsibility to the widow and orphan. Luke's congregation or community would have been familiar with this expectation. Many would have identified with the poor, the blind and the oppressed because they saw themselves in this way.

13.　The term 'kingdom of God' is challenged today from both a feminist theological position and because of its connection with monarchy. A more appropriate term may be reign or Community of God.

14.　Trainor, Johnson, Fitzymer, *op cit.*

The rich and powerful would be expected to bring the good news of God's kingdom by forgiving debt and sharing with the poor. This concern for the marginalised and the poor is to be a reflection of God's own generosity and mercy.

In Luke's vision of the kingdom, the poor, the powerless and the marginalised are to be affirmed while the powerful are brought low. Luke's kingdom is about the way in which human life and God can interrelate, of what could be. God's kingdom is not about a servant-master relationship, but about mutual sharing and interdependence. It is to be a non-hierarchic kingdom which is demonstrated in the way a community expresses concern for the poor and the marginalised. This is a community where relationships are central to its functioning.

In contrast to Matthew's account of the Sermon on the Mount, Luke's story takes place after a mountain-top experience. Jesus comes down into the marketplace to join his disciples and 'a great multitude of people from all Judea, Jerusalem and the coast of Tyre and Sidon' surround him.[15]

From these words, it appears that the crowd was a mixture of rich and poor, Jews, gentiles and pagans. Luke's Jesus predicts the likelihood of turbulence in the days to come as he engages the crowd with his message of God's justice. Jesus warns his intimate followers that the road ahead will not be easy and points to the suffering likely to be experienced.

His words are pointers to the suffering that is to be experienced on the way, an indicator of the cost of discipleship. These words speak of costly love, essential in understanding God's kingdom, a kingdom that has a special preference for the poor and the marginalised and one that is present, yet can only be fulfilled according to God's generous spirit.

In contrast to the other Gospel writers, Luke's kingdom is proclaimed as a present reality. The implication is that the building of community is the responsibility of all who seek to

---

15.   Luke 6:17

walk in the footsteps of Jesus. Sharing in this task is both a privilege and a responsibility. For Luke the time is now, and every opportunity should be taken to address existing inequalities and tensions in community life. This is what Luke understands as enacting the traditions, the principles of Jubilee, rather than being preoccupied with a future heavenly expectation of judgment. It is what could be described as a present eschatology, challenging the injustices of present community life.

7.7 Justice and jubilee

Luke, in his account of the kingdom of God is revisiting the content of Jewish scripture, using pre 70 CE teaching to present his theme. The year of jubilee features prominently in Lukan teaching on the kingdom. Jubilee is a time for 'release' and the 'year of the Lord.'[16]

Jubilee is a time for liberation and review of the covenant relationship. Jubilee is a reflection of Luke's understanding of God's righteousness *sdaqah* and justice *mishpat*, which speaks of the restoration of the relationship with God on the basis of God's generosity, God's grace. Luke's justice, which underpins God's kingdom, is a statement of the corporate responsibility of the people of God. Luke recalls Israel's memory, particularly the faithfulness and justice of God, as experienced in the Exodus account. Justice is therefore a community concern and responsibility. Forgiveness, remission of debts, openness and compassion are central to both its meaning and expression. The idea that human fulfilment is achieved through a sense of mutual interdependence and the generous outpourings of God's grace provides evidence of the continuing interest of the divine in the whole of creation. Luke's use of jubilee is again illustrative of his reversal motif.

---

16. *Ibid*, 81, illustrates how Luke draws heavily on passages from Isaiah announcing good news to the poor. He goes on to state that some readers see words such as 'release' and 'year of the Lord' portraying Jesus as announcing the eschatological Jubilee year. Further references to Jubilee may be found in the *New Bible Dictionary* (Leicester, England: Inter Varsity Press, 1986).

8. Summary

The approach of Luke in his interpretation of Jesus provides an authoritative foundation for developing and defining what may be a distinctive role for church welfare agencies. Luke's concern for the poor and the marginalised and his understanding of key theological principles underpinning the promises of God's kingdom, strengthens and provides the authority for a strong advocacy role for agencies.

In particular, Luke's Sermon on the Plain, as in fact does his whole Gospel, provides a strong theological and scriptural starting point for defining and interpreting the agency's role in the postmodern era.

A distinctively Christian role for agencies within a broader justice context will centre around the life and ministry of Jesus, and His story should enhance and inform the role of agencies. From this perspective, the agencies can present a world view alternative to the current market paradigm—a world view which encapsulates a commitment to God's justice and Christian hope, not only for the poor and marginalised, but one which embraces the whole of creation. The task here is to establish and articulate social goals which correlate with the economic agenda. An agenda which sets forth a vision that seeks to utilise and distribute the world's resources in a way which ensures proper housing, health, education and income for everyone so that all may reach their potential.

A distinctive Christian understanding of creation embodies a belief in our common humanity, communion in its fullest sense. Structures and policies which diminish the human person, marginalise or exploit should be challenged. Building a just community is not the same as managing or psychologising the poor. Instead a just community is about rights and relationships and responsibility.

A View from the Church Agency Perspective

Marilyn Webster

Love... Compassion.... Justice... Mercy... The poor... The lame... The least in the community: these are the gospel values which underpin the mission of the church through its community service agencies.

Accountability... Effectiveness... Efficiency... Best value, The consumer... The individual: these are the market values which underpin the mission of the market through community services.

The role of the church in providing community services, and particularly the relationship with the government as 'purchaser' of services has confronted workers and administrators of church-based services with a particular set of challenges. The extent to which these challenges have been seen as a threat to the core mission of church community services has really depended on how that mission has been portrayed.

In the 1990's, with the application of a contractualist approach to the management of their relationship with government, agencies have been shocked into a re-examination of what is fundamental to the content and process of their work. This 'shock' of grappling with an environment of which is variously called the economic rationalist approach, neo-liberalism, market capitalism or market liberalism has exposed workers and agencies in a new way. We have a sense of what that has meant for church agencies and the people we work with but the pace of change has been so rapid, and the agencies found to be so under-resourced in dealing with it, that engagement with some of the wider questions of the market and the church has been difficult. This is a shame because there are issues of justice here which go the core of agencies' work. It is vitally important that we in the church community services lean on the work of our theologians to assist us in making sense of these pressures.

Responses by church agencies themselves have been varied, from one of enthusiastic engagement with the contractual state to one of profound reluctance to acknowledge changed circumstances.

In 1993 the Australian Catholic Social Welfare Commission described the challenges thus:

> The welfare sector is in the midst of change. It is being subjected to an enforced identity change and the adoption of market values that are the antithesis of the values that underpin not-for-profit services to the community. Government bureaucratic practice, if not deliberate government policy, is shifting from providing broad-based subsidies in a spirit of cooperation and partnership to the use of market constructs such as contracts, tendering, versions of voucher arrangements, the encouragement of fee for service structures, outcome performance indicators and quality control structures. These contracts are leading to a model of non-government welfare service stripped of its own values, identity and autonomy. Like market franchise systems, services would simply mirror a corporate identity, value base and service.[1]

In many senses this vision has come to pass. We really do have a McDonalds community service system and many church agencies may be reluctant participants, but they are participating.

---

1. Australian Catholic Social Welfare Commission, *Market Principles and Welfare: the dilemmas of privatizing Australia's welfare services* (Sydney: Australian Catholic Social Welfare Commission, 1993).

Some of the issues for church-based community service agencies in this new environment include the following inter-related issues considered by Good Shepherd in its response, not only to a contractualised environment of government funded services, but also to approaches by privatised and corporatised entities concerning participation in service provision.

1. State, Church and Business
The question of whether church-based agencies can, or should, participate in a contractualised service system displaces real debate about the consequences of buying into areas once the preserve of government. As the State draws back church agencies need to ask why we are stepping into the void.

The works of church agencies have traditionally arisen because needs of people who are not provided for, either by government or the market, have been identified and responded to. The consequences of assisting in the creation of a marketised community service system may not be known for many years, but a real concern is that church agencies may be assisting in the erosion of what has become known as 'social capital'—that complex of participation, volunteerism and association.

As well, church-based agencies might be contributing to the erosion of legitimacy for government responsibility in areas of social need. This moves beyond the argument over 'efficiency of service delivery' to 'legitimacy of service delivery'. While church agencies may be just as efficient in delivering services, one needs to ask what the long-term effects may be. Some responses to social need require greater elements of social control, statutory provision, standardised service provisions and a means of dispassionately assessing entitlement to service. A service should also be characterised by notions of equity and justice as these values allow for appropriate appeals and review processes. In order to achieve these in a marketised system government must introduce elements of rigidity and control over community services, including in their relationships with church agencies, and often these controls may not produce fairness or equity. Examples where there have been particular difficulties have been the employment services and the role of church agencies in 'breaching', or the provision of health services for the prison system.

2. Maintenance of Mission

Good Shepherd sees its primary role as providing support and care for people who are poor and marginalised and we do this by being in relationship with them. This develops the imagery of service, of the Good Shepherd who leads and protects the sheep. The Good Shepherd vision and mission has equally been the Good Shepherd with the crook beating off the wolves. This is developed in the work of justice, seeking to ensure that those who are exploited, marginalised and vulnerable are at the centre of advocacy and actively supported in social change to achieve social and economic rights. These twin motivations of both 'charity' and 'justice' are made very real to the workers of Good Shepherd through comprehensive orientation programs, agency-wide days and in engagement with decisions about programs.

The creation of community through the provision of service has been given a high priority by Good Shepherd programs and much effort has been expended by the agency to engage workers in community building actions through direct service (ie support and counselling) work. This approach has always been part of the Good Shepherd approach but a conscious strategy was developed in the mid 1990s, largely in response to the pressures of contracting. In particular, it was a response to the redevelopment of Youth and Family Services which, while attempting to address some major system concerns around the visibility and accessibility of youth and family services in Victoria, threatened to undermine the capacity for enhancement of community connectedness for those using Good Shepherd services.

As well as reiterating the commitment of Good Shepherd to community building as integral to the work of the agency, a code for assessing whether or not the agency should be considering to tender for a particular service was developed. This code emphasised the congruence of the agencies' traditional areas of work for families and young people, and the capacity to retain integrity with respect to community engagement and relationship development with the families and individuals being assisted. This code was developed by the staff of the agency in the context of a review of mission and strategic directions, and prevented a drift away from core expertise and mission in the search for funding to ensure continuity of the agency. It is difficult now to appreciate how real this threat to continuity was for various agencies, and how isolating such a course could be.

3. An Understanding of Partnership

One of the problems for agencies in the church sector during the contracting era has been co-option of the language of which the sector has traditionally used to express what it is doing and how it does it. The notion of 'partnership' is one example of this. Traditionally, both government and the sector have described the arrangement by which government provided block funding, and agencies delivered services as a 'partnership'. At the height of contractualism in the Victorian community services sector the 'partnership' took on the demeanour of a full developed business 'partnership' under-pinned by 'contract'.

However the Funding and Service Agreements (FASA's) suffered many of the failings identified by Oslington. These failings have been closely examined in a recent report of the Public Accounts and Estimates Committee.[2]

Clearly agencies did not enter arrangements as a fully autonomous partner. The sole 'purchaser' of the services, the Department of Human Services had a number of additional goals. Some of these were the reduction of the number of agencies providing funded services, system redesign through enforced service coalitions and contraction, and co-option of the broad service system to the 'core' government responsibilities of child protection. There was no agreement on measures of

---

2. Public Accounts and Estimates Committee, Victorian Parliament, 2002.

quality of service. Adequate measures of the quality of service are notoriously difficult to identify, particularly in the child and family services area. Change is often incremental and not focused within 'episodes' of care. A surrogate measure often utilised in the area is the client satisfaction survey but this is insufficient as a measure of quality of service.

4. The Changing Character of the Workforce

Good Shepherd has had an extremely stable workforce. As a small agency, it attracts the altruistic and highly motivated workforce identified by Oslington. The rise of contractualism has meant that the commitment of many workers can only last as long as the agency's commitment to them; ie employment is guaranteed until the end of the contract. The end of the contract brings anxiety and concern for the future. Efforts turn to contract renewal rather than service delivery, and there is an immense task for management to maintain optimism and focus on the primary relationships with those being supported through the work of the agency. There is concern for those using the services: an extremely vulnerable group unlikely or unable to exercise choice of another service in the event of a service closing.

To some, service closure has always occurred in the sector and there has been an impact on these being served, often in a pilot or demonstration project. Core family and child support services, however, are severely impacted because of confused service pathways and disruption of local networks and these can take many years to recover.

The period of contractualism in Victoria, with its associated constraining of costs, has seen an increasing gap in wage rates for the so-called 'voluntary' sector including the church-based agencies. For church-based agencies accustomed to a vocational workforce and a history of voluntarism, justice in wage rates has always been a difficult issue. These agencies are particularly vulnerable to the pressures from government to be part of the 'McDonalds' service system. Those that do not participate will have a declining capacity to pay and to attract staff, however altruistic in intent.

5. Identifying and Serving Need

The church-based community service agencies have traditionally seen themselves as innovators in responding to emerging areas of disadvantage in the community. For a very long time it was possible for agencies such as Good Shepherd to fund these innovations through direct donation or by persuading government that existing funding could be redirected, or indeed by redirecting money without consultation. The recognised tension between the need for more accountability, transparency and legitimate control over the agency's purpose and direction is a very real one.

David deCarvalho, drawing on the analogy of a Greek trireme, describes this tension as to whether the church agency will be 'steering, not rowing'.[3] The extent to which the church-based agency is able to maintain its hand on the tiller depends on the capacity to renew core mission while at the same time retaining sufficient independence in resources to ensure that it is able to redirect efforts into areas which do not attract the interest of government.

For many agencies, including Good Shepherd, this has required a re-examination of those government funded services which are provided: do they indeed reflect a preference for the 'poor' or has the agency's provision of service merely continued a historical association?

6. Maintaining a Holistic Approach

One of the key challenges for agencies has been to resist the partialisation of response which comes with the service descriptions attached to contracting. It is impossible to describe the dimension of human need and the response to it within a service contract but Good Shepherd has attempted to maintain a holistic approach in the support it gives to individuals and families approaching the agency. This is often described as

---

3.   De Carvalho, David, *Steering not Rowing*, paper presented to The Markets and Church, a forum of Catholic Social Services, the Salvation Army and the Uniting Church, May 1995, Melbourne.

'value adding' and is the very thing that is attractive to governments seeking to engage the church sector in service delivery. There is a point at which the church-based community service agencies are wary of this attraction because it has the potential to undermine the very linkages they seek to bring to their work with families. Rabbi Sacks reported in Curti describes these as 'intermediate "third-sector" institutions: families, faith communities and neighbourhoods held together by love, loyalty and faithfulness. If these were missing there would be difficulties neither governments nor the markets could solve'. [4]

The reality is that for many of those being supported by Good Shepherd, these things are missing and it is the capacity to provide both sense of community and skills in community living, as well as the access to the intermediate community institutions which comprises the holistic approach of the agency.

7. Notions of Community and Shared Responsibility

One element of the contractual approach to community service provision which has been particularly difficult for church community service agencies like Good Shepherd is the attempt to define the dimensions of responsibility for service to people within the confines of a contractual agreement. There has been much experimentation with different forms of the funding and service agreement in Victoria. What is of concern here is how shared responsibility for vulnerable people in the community is described.

What is most easily described is the government obligation to areas of statutory responsibility. A second area easily described is the dimension of service provision funded by government. These areas are largely characterised primarily by tertiary and residual attempts to assist people who the community has failed. This concentration of effort and expenditure in these areas has led, over a period of time, to a weakening of those preventative service options which are

---

4.   Curti, Elena, *God and Government*, The Tablet 2000. www.thetablet.co.uk/reports

often delivered locally and which can be community streng-thening.

In Victoria there has been recognition of the weakening of community bonds as a result of the impact of marketisation with extensive efforts by government to turn this around with major initiatives in community building and early childhood service development. However, the concentration of community services through mergers and acquisitions makes the larger church community service organisation less responsive at a local level. To a certain extent we in the church agencies are suffering the same remoteness and lack of responsiveness to community that government promised would be addressed by privatised service provision.

8. The Longer Term

It is important that the shift to competitive tendering and the marketisation of welfare is seen in the context of an evolving relationship of government and church through its community service agencies. The changes in the relationship have been marked by competitive tendering and through a number of different funding mechanisms applied by government over a period of time. Thus it is too simplistic to assume that drawing back from competitive tendering will avoid the fundamental questions for church agencies.

Nowland-Forman[5] states that the pattern of development of the government funding relationship has generally moved through a number of (largely) sequential stages with competitive tendering only one of a number of steps to individualised service purchasing:

---

5.   Nowland-Forman, Garth, *Wise as Serpents, Gentle as Doves – being real about what's at stake in NGOs and Governments working together effectively*, paper presented to Commonwealth/Regional Workshop for Pacific, Navigating the Pacific: exploring NGO/Government Co-operation in a Changing World, Papkur Marae, Auckland/Tamaki-makau-ratu, 24-28 February 1997.

a. donations to worthwhile organisations (list approach)
b. program grants in response to submissions (submission models);
c. program grants allocated on the basis of some form of service planning (needs-based planning);
d. tendering for contracts to undertake specified services (purchase of service contracting);
e. funding to individuals to purchase services from accredited providers (vouchers) or the market (cash allowances).

While the ultimate goal in the market approach might be to give power to the consumer over individual purchase of service decisions, in fact it is the government expectations of, and potential for, control of community service organisations, including church organisations, which increase with the sophistication of the funding mechanism.

It emerges that the government and church community service organisations have been engaged in this process for many years. It began with the initial provision of government funding for services and while we don't know how long the current phase might last or what the landscape might look like when we leave the tunnel, we can know with certainty that the relationship with government will have irretrievably impacted on community service agencies.

What is less certain is whether having a choice of service is sufficient to guarantee justice for individuals in the human services area. A review of the employment services privatisation undertaken by the Organisation for Economic Co-operation and Development found that the one significant difference between the government-provided system and the privatised system was that of efficiency. The privatised system was cheaper to run—but at the same time concerns were expressed at the outcomes for those on the margins.

Questions for Group Discussion

QUESTIONS FOR GROUP DISCUSSION IN CHURCHES

1. Can you identify any underlying issues in Paul Oslington's paper? Do you think they are at variance with values in Ray Cleary's?

2. Do we need specific biblical endorsement (chapter and verse) of the theological ideas in Ray Cleary's and Marilyn Webster's papers? How can we get from text to theology?

3. Can you agree on the basic moral principles about contracting-out of welfare services? Does that imply that church agencies, in accepting contracts from Governments, are doing the work of government and losing their own values in the provision and quality of services?

4. How do you, as a member of a local church, learn about the work and concerns of your local church agencies? Do you, as a church member in your local community, have a role in caring for other members of that community? How do/would you exercise that role?

5. Is there a role for members of the local community to advocate for change with and for the poor and marginalised in your community? How would you find a way to give expression to your concerns?

QUESTIONS FOR STAFF OF CHURCH WELFARE AGENCIES:

[For this discussion, it would be useful to have available your agency's Mission Statement and any other existing public statement on agency values.]

1. Do you think Christian values get in the way of professionalism? Do you have examples of this?

2.   Do the papers by Ray Cleary and Marilyn Webster lead you in the direction of opposing contracting out of community services?

3.   Do you think your agency's values are under threat when it accepts government contracts?

The Authors

The Hon Brian Howe was variously Health Minister, Minister for Social Security and Deputy Prime Minister in the Hawke and Keating Governments in Australia in the 1980s and 90s. Before being elected to Parliament, he was a Uniting Church ordained minister in Melbourne, and following his retirement from politics, resumed ministry. He is a Professor in the Centre for Public Policy in the University of Melbourne.

Paul Oslington is Senior Lecturer in Economics, Australian Defence Force Academy within the University of New South Wales, and a Visiting Fellow at St Marks National Theological Centre in Canberra. After completing a PhD in economics at University of Sydney and BD from Melbourne College of Divinity, his research has focused on the economics of international trade and unemployment, and relationships between economics and religion. Papers on economics and religion have appeared in *History of Economics Review, History of Political Economy, International Journal of Social Economics* and an survey volume *The State of Economic Science*. A student reading guide 'Christianity and Economics' was recently published by the Zadok Institute for Christianity and Society and edited volume *Economics and Religion* in the Elgar International Library of Critical Writings in Economics is forthcoming.

He may be contacted at the School of Economics and Management, Australian Defence Force Academy, Northcott Drive, Canberra ACT 2600, Australia.
Email: p.oslington@adfa.edu.au.

Canon Ray Cleary, BEcon, BSW, BTheol, DMin, is chief executive of Anglicare Victoria, a large welfare service provider. He has a Doctor of Ministry degree from the United Faculty of Theology, Melbourne, with a thesis on justice and welfare services. He is a Canon of St Paul's Anglican Cathedral, Melbourne.

The

Marilyn Webster, BA, BSW, is social policy officer for Good Shepherd Youth and Family Services, Melbourne. She previously held senior social work positions in the Mission of St James and St John and Jesuit Social Services Melbourne.

Alan Nichols, MA (Theol) is an Anglican priest and consultant based in Melbourne. He is a Senior Fellow in the Centre for Applied Philosophy and Public Ethics, University of Melbourne.

Maureen Postma, BA (Hons) is General Secretary of the Victorian Council of Churches, Melbourne.

DATE DUE